AUTHENTIC INSIGHTS

By

CECELIA FRANCES PAGE

iUniverse, Inc.
New York   Bloomington

i

Authentic Insights

iUniverse books may be ordered through booksellers or by contacting:

*iUniverse
1663 Liberty Drive
Bloomington, IN 47403
www.iuniverse.com
1-800-Authors (1-800-288-4677)*

*ISBN: 978-1-4502-5820-3 (sc)
ISBN: 978-1-4502-5821-0 (ebook)*

Printed in the United States of America

iUniverse rev. date: 09/17/2010

Table of Contents

PREFACE

AUTHENTIC INSIGHTS is a book of extraordinary experiences and events. There are 70, stimulating short stories and articles to enjoy and appreciate. HUMAN INTEREST topics are 89 Year-Old Woman Hiked Across the U.S.A. Be Yourself, Unusual Occasions, About Laura Ingles Wilder, Who's Who In The Film Industry, Art Linkletter, Broadcaster, Author and Entrepreneur and About Jerry Brown As A California Governor.

ADVENTURE topics, are Amazing Wonders, Splendid Occurrences Rare Moments Seafarers, Lasting Memories, Miracles, The Hidden Treasures, Imagine If You Could Fly, At Midstream, Traveling On An Amtrak Train, and Rambling On.

PHILOSOPHICAL AND RELIGIOUS topics are Natural Living, About The Secret Doctrine, Be Yourself, Harmonious Times, Unusual Perspectives, Authentic Insights, The Kolbrin Bible, Be Thankful, Be Charitable, Sedona, A Spiritual Place, A Better Way Of Living and How Religion Affects People.

SCIENTIFIC, NATURE and HEALING topics are Planet X Forecast and More about 2012, Four Million Year Old Computer Baffles Scientists, Garlic, The Great Healer, Natural Living, Preparing Gourmet Food, The Spectacular Garden, The Amethyst Stones, Lemurs Survive In Madagascar, The Meadowlark, Oceans And Seas On Earth, Massage Techniques, Marvels And Wonders, Avoid Unnecessary Toxins, Healing Herb Remedies, Evolution Of The Earth, Chocolate Can Heal You.

CULTURAL and POLITICAL topics are About Jerry Brown As California Governor, The European Renaissance, Mysteries Of The Ancient World, Books, Books, And More Books, Amazing Wonders,

New Age Education, Political Issues That Concern American Citizens, The Persian Culture and Siberia – Vast Land In Russia.

MUSIC and ART TOPICS are Mosaic Designs, Well Known Operas, Decorate Your Home With A Christmas Tree, Choral Presentations, Using Different Pencils And Pens and The Doll House.

OTHER TOPICS are Hand Held Google Translator, The Paranormal Travels Of Mark Twain, Why We Should Keep Alert, The Lighthouse, The Narrow Escape, Use Your Imagination, Santa Clause Is Coming To Town, Original Poems, Galactic Awareness and Cobblestone Roads.

ABOUT THE AUTHOR

Cecelia Frances Page has a B.A. and M.A. in Education. She also focused in English, Speech, Drama, Psychology and Music. Cecelia is a prolific writer of original poems, screenplays, novels and nonfiction books. Forty-four of Cecelia's books are published by iUniverse Incorporated. Cecelia has published five, original screenplays and three, original poetry books. Cecelia Frances Page is an educator, author, drama director, pianist, vocal soloist, artist, photographer and philosopher. Cecelia Frances Page continues to write worthwhile and inspirational books. She has written 52 books.

Novels written by Cecelia Frances Page are *WESTWARD PURSUIT, IMAGINE IF...,OPPORTUNE TIMES, MYSTICAL REALITIES, BRILLIANT CANDOR, SEEK ENLIGHTENMENT WITHIN, CELESTIAL CONNECTIONS, CELESTIAL BEINGS FROM OUTER SPACE, PATHWAYS TO SELF REALIZATION, MAGNIFICENT CELESTIAL JOURNEYS, EXTRAORDINARY ENCOUNTERS, HORIZONS BEYOND, PHENOMENAL EXPERIENCES, ADVENTURES ON ANCIENT CONTINENTS and FORTUNATELY.*

Philosophical and Religious Books are *AWAKEN TO SPIRITUAL ILLUMINATION, EXPAND YOUR AWARENESS AND VIVID MEMORIES OF HALCYON.*

Cecelia Frances Page's Short Stories and Articles are: *INCREDIBLE TIMES, FASCINATING TOPICS, INTERPRETATIONS OF LIFE, ADVENTUROUS EXPERIENCES, MARVELOUS REFLECTIONS, STIMULATING AWARENESS ABOUT LIFE, MAGNIFICENT RECOLLECTIONS. TANGIBLE REALITIES, REMARKABLE WORLD TRAVELS, THR FUTURE AGE BEYOND THE NEW AGE MOVEMENT, INFINITE OPPORTUNITIES, IMMENSE*

PROBABILITIES, SIGNIFICANT MOMENTS, MIRACULOUS WONDERS, AUTHENTIC INSIGHTS and more.

To purchase Cecelia Frances Page's books contact Cecelia Frances Page, author at iUniverse Incorporated.com, Call 1-800-288-4677 Extension 5025 at the Book Order Department,

ONE

THE EUROPEAN RENAISSANCE

During the Middle Ages from 1400 A.D. to 1600 A.D. ENTERPRISING MEN WERE ABLE TO MAKE GREAT FORTUNES. As a result, a new Middle Class of prosperous merchants emerged in cities and towns. Italy was the most civilized country in Europe. Merchants brought luxuries from the East to sell to the countries of Northern Europe. They brought back wool, timber, wheat, hides and silk goods by sea carrier to his agents into the major European ports.

Italians devised a bill of exchange, a note authorizing payment at an office in one country from money received in another. They also invented double, entry bookkeeping to record such transactions. By making trade easier and accounting more accurate, these methods laid the foundation of modern commerce.

Some Italian merchant families became very rich and powerful during the European Renaissance. They lent money to the kings of Europe who were patrons of the great Renaissance artists. A certain merchant of Prato near Florence, Francisco di Marco Datino, who started as a poor innkeeper's son, went to France to make his fortune in Avignon. Avignon was a great international trading center. He established two flourishing import and export companies and three shops.

Francisco di Marco Datino built a beautiful, big, new house in Prato, which was built of plastered brick with painted decorations

1

inside and out. His house had an enclosed courtyard with a well. The house had an open colonnade for entertaining on each floor. The upper floor served for drying clothes. Behind the house were a beautiful garden and a warehouse containing Francisco's main office. The brick floors were polished and waxed.

Prato was a cloth making town. Francisco's wealth and foreign contacts enabled him to import fine wool cloth abroad. His real fortune was made in luxury goods and spices. Francisco bought farmland where he built a villa and houses for the farm workers. The farm produced wheat, wine, olives and fresh produce for the Prato households. Gradually, Francisco bought up other plots of land until he had 300 acres of orchards and farms. Many tenants rented the land.

The landowner supplied the farm and equipment and the peasants labored on the land. They shared the profit equally according to the mezzalera system.

The English manor house of the fifteenth century was more comfortable and convenient than its predecessors. The strength of a feudal overlord had formerly depended on the loyalty of his men, whom in return, he had protected against a hostile world.

Cathay Manor in Somerset, England, clearly shows how an up-to-date country house of the time was planned. Cathay's hall had a fashionable minstrel. Wealthy people had window glass. Walls were hung with painted cloths for warmth. The very rich had wooden paneling, or tapestry, called the Arras after the Burgundian town where much of it was made. Furniture and clothes were influenced by the elegant courts of France and Burgundy.

By 1500, three sheep existed for every human being in England. Thrifty peasants had been accumulating blocks of land by buying additional strips from other peasants or exchanging with their neighbors. A man who owned eighty or so acres could cultivate them using the labor of his family and produce enough for his support and a surplus to sell in the town. He could afford to build a fine timber farmstead with a hall and parlor. The English countryside was soon developed with prosperous farmsteads of new, independent, Yeoman farmers.

Southern Germany was one of the first regions outside of Italy to receive new ideas which excited Italian artists and scholars in the fifteenth century. Its craftsmen excelled as armorers, goldsmiths, silversmith and jewelers. Stimulated by the rediscovery of Greek mathematics they sought to establish the exact nature of the universe by astronomical observations.

The development of printing with woodblock printing on textiles was used to create printed books. Paper making which the Arabs learned from the Chinese was brought to Europe in the twelfth century. Paper making was widely used by the fifteenth century. Large scale publishing first became established among the metal workers of Nuremberg.

German metal workers of the fifteenth century increased the amount of metal available and made better quality cast iron by using larger blast furnaces with huge water-powered bellows. Metal tools and machine parts came into use. Bronze founders perfected their technique in casting church bells.

Europe became a dominant world power. Nuremburg's rapid increase in prosperity is expressed in many books of etiquette produced in the fifteenth century. By 1500 nearly every family had its own house. Nuremburg's surrounding land guaranteed supplies of all the food the townspeople needed.

Gifts of money from wealthy citizens established all sorts of charitable institutions for the sick and needy. The Mendel Almshouse, founded in 1388, provided free board and lodging for retired master craftsmen. Two masters from each craft were responsible to the city council for the testing of every object before it could be sold.

From medieval times England acquired its wealth from the quality of its raw wool, which was exported all over Europe. East Anglia was the chief cloth-producing region and Lavenham in Suffolk its most important center. The half-timbered framed houses were the substantial homes of its wealthy cloth manufacturers. Timber was still the accepted building material. Brick chimneys provided fireproof blues. They also housed internal ovens and provided hearths to warm the houses.

Spain and Portugal were the first European countries to create a systematic policy of discovery. They discovered sea routes to the favored trade lands of eastern Asia. Columbus landed in the Americas in 1492. He believed that he had landed in China. The Spaniard Balboa crossed the Isthmus of Panama in 1513 and he was the first European to see the Pacific Ocean. Spain acquired enough gold and silver to make Spain the greatest power in Europe. Spanish fashions and manners were copied. Spain was a cultural leader. A new university at Alcal de Henares, became one of Europe's finest universities.

Spanish writers and painters of this period, Lapede Vegas, Cervantes, El Greco and Velazquez, are among the greatest of all time. Renaissance enthusiasm, along with the combination of gold and silver from the New World, led to new building of new churches, hospital, town halls and houses for the rich.

The Renaissance in Europe was between 1400 and 1600. During the Middle Ages people worked on farms. In towns, craftsmen were organized into guilds which controlled all aspects of production and distribution. Society was dominated by wealthy noblemen and large landowners. Religious and intellectual life was centered in the Church. During the Renaissance people felt a need for changes to be made.

As society slowly evolved into the Renaissance, people began to rediscover the writings of Plato and Aristotle from Greece. In the arts, as sculptors studied the statues of Greece and Rome they began to create more lifelike works. Artists stopped painting portraits and landscapes in perspective. In literature began to write books about the ideal citizen. Authors began to write about what really happened in every day life in their own countries. They used their native language instead of Latin. Those in the upper classes enjoyed themselves with singing the latest madrigals and eating well.

The Renaissance was a time of great scientific and technological discoveries. Astronomers observed the skies and constellations. They learned that the Earth is round and it revolves around the Sun. Thinkers and writers studied how people interact with each other. In several Italian cities they formed clubs (camerata) in which they discussed some of the ideas (such as the "dignity of man" which, hundreds of years later, helped form the basis of our Declaration of Independence and Constitution.

Renaissance means "rebirth." With the printing of inexpensive books, education became more available throughout Europe. "Books formerly rare and dear, have become common and easy to procure," stated Layse Le Toy, the French writer in his book THE EXCELLENCE OF THIS AGE.

Some influential people who lived during the Renaissance are Leonardo da Vinci (Italy), Luther (Germany), Eramus (Holland), Copernicus (Poland), Columbus (Spain), Michelangelo (Italy), and many more people. A famous teacher, Viltarino, started his own school. His aim was to develop the body, mind and soul of his students. He became known as one of the greatest humanist teachers in Europe. Many of Viltarino's students became extraordinary civic and Church leaders in Italy. Federigo da Montefeltro, Duke of Urbino was one of Viltarino's students. He contributed a great library.

Leonardo da Vinci from Italy was the most brilliant inventor and one of the greatest artists of the Renaissance. Leonardo da Vinci was also an architect, sculptor, musician, astronomer and town planner. He designed engineering projects in the fields of hydraulics, ship building, military, structural and mechanical engineering. He studied anatomy, biology, zoology, botany, geology, geography, and mathematics. Leonardo da Vinci made 5000 pages of drawings. He illustrated new ways of looking at plants, skeletons and muscles. He sketched diving helmets, steam engines, pumps, cranes, etc. He was the first to design an airplane, a helicopter, a military tank and a machine gun. He worked for Ludovico Sforza. Leonardo da Vinci designed costumes and stage machinery for the lavish entertainments.

As an artist, Leonardo da Vinci was best known for painting the MONA LISA, which now hangs in the Louvre Museum in Paris. His ideas were so far ahead of his time that most of the people of the Renaissance did not understand them. His scientific and anatomical discoveries were not published until long after his death.

Michelangelo Buonarotli from Italy was another influential genius of the Renaissance as a sculptor, painter, architect and poet. At the age of 14 he was apprenticed to a leading artist. Larengo de Medici was interested in Michelangelo's many talents. So, Michelangelo was invited to stay at the Medici household. While he lived there he became acquainted with the leading intellectuals of Florence, known as Ficino, Landinovrend Paliziano. Hundreds of Michelangelo's original poems and poetic fragments have survived, some as lyrics set to music by well known composers.

Michelangelo's best known sculpture is the huge figure of DAVID which was placed outside the Paloazzo Vecchio in Florence. His most famous paintings are in the Sistine Chapel in Rome. He was commissioned to paint the vaulted ceiling. He recreated the Biblical story from the creation to Noah. Behind the altar he painted THE LAST JUDGMENT, one of the most emotion-filled works even to be seen according to Lee McRae, who wrote HANDBOOK OF THE RENAISSANCE.

Lorenzo De Medici, from Italy, guided Florence to become the cultural center of the Western world. He was patron to those extraordinary artists, Michelangelo, Botticelli and Leonardo da Vinci. Lorenao was a wise diplomat, a scholar, athlete, millionaire, musician and poet. He was a banker. He was a ruler of Florence and represented Florence in times of war. He was referred as "Lorenzo the Magnificent." He helped to prevent a war between Naples and Florence when he went unarmed to negotiate with King Ferrante of Naples.

Martin Luther, from Germany, was a priest who protested openly against the Catholic Church granting indulgences in order to raise money to build a new cathedral in Rome. He wrote many pamphlets criticizing the Church's wealth and hypocrisy. He drew up 95 demands for reform and he nailed these to the door of the castle chapel in Wittenberg. Because of his protests the Protestant Church was established. He translated the Bible into the German language. He became the best selling writer of his country once the printing press was invented. Martin Luther's impact has lasted until today," said Le McRae.

Nicholas Copernicus, from Poland, was a priest, who studied about the universe, and claimed that the Earth revolved around the Sun. He could not speak about his ideas and thoughts because they were contrary to the beliefs of the Catholic Church. Copernicus had a book published about his new beliefs in 1543. He was called "father of astronomy" because of his conclusions on the nature of the stars and planets.

Desiderius Erasmus, from Holland, hoped to change the Catholic Church with reason and persuasion through his writings. Some of his books questioned the Catholic Church. He became friends with the great printer, Aldus Mahutius who helped increase Erasmus' fame by publishing his works. His writings included the scholarly translation of the NEW TESTAMENT from Greek into Latin. His satiric wit in books such as THE PRAISE OF FOLLY and COLLOQUIES became best sellers. "It was through his books that he became known as a beloved and leading humanist of Northern Europe", said Lee McRae,

Francois Rabelais, from France, was an independent thinker, lawyer, priest, physician and writer. As a doctor, he believed that a simple diet, laughter and joy could cure some illnesses. His most outrageous stories were about GARGANTUA and PANTAGRUEL known as a "hymn to the Renaissance."

The European Renaissance was a time for reawakening and better opportunities and changes. Literature, new inventions, the Arts and Science flourished and continued to develop and expand in Europe. Influential people mentioned in this Renaissance era made a difference in making significant differences in cultural and technological changes in the world.

TWO

FOUR MILLION YEAR OLD COMPUTER BAFFLES SCIENTISTS

Scientists are amazed that computers existed four million years ago by the lost civilization of Atlantis. The archaeological discovery of an ancient computer made entirely of crystal is boggling scientists, who say it is far superior to space age technology," said Julie Golden." Records found in the excavated computer have convinced some researchers that it was built by ancient engineers from Atlantis, the legendary, advanced civilization although to have been destroyed by a flood millions of years ago," Julie Golden claims. Individuals who have created computers in the 20th and 21st centuries may have subconscious memories traced back to ancient civilizations like Atlantis.

Julie Golden stated that, "the staggering find was unearthed last year during an archaeological expedition headed by Linda Waldren, an expert in ancient civilizations." Waldron conducted investigations over 25 years. Waldren believes the ancient Atlantean civilization existed at the island of Bimini off the coast of Florida. This island is the tip of one of the world's largest underwater mountains.

Linda Walden told the EXAMINER that she had excavated an underwater region off Bimini "where several artifacts previously had been found at the opening of a sealed-off cavern." She gained access into a cave during her trip which turned out to be a 30-foot high, domelike hall. There was a flat, table-like structure made of solid gems across an unusual set with pink and green markings that are very similar to the laser bar price coding used at supermarket check-out counters," claims Linda Waldron, a New York researcher. "The object began to give off a high pitched frequency that eventually became inaudible to her hearing" stated Linda Waldren.

This object began to transmit information. It turned out to be consistent with geographical data on volcano eruptions occurring in the area more than five million years ago. The physicist who accompanied the expedition said, "We've never seen anything like it before. The computer memory is formed by the pattern of the crystal and is virtually indestructible. The records have been preserved."

Crystal lasts because it is durable and very solid. Crystal is not used in modern computers. However, the fact that computers have come back into existence in modern times is phenomenal. The ancient computer is activated by a touch-sensitive mechanism charged with solar power and contains a kind of artificial intelligence that interacts with known brain waves." It literally reads your thoughts and transmits the information requested directly into your brain," Linda Waldren said.

Scientists have compared the find with the discovery of the Rosetta Stone, which unlocked the secrets of ancient Egypt. "Now we can finally learn the secrets of the last civilization of Atlantis," Linda Waldron said. Perhaps we can learn from this ancient Atlantean civilization how to avoid destroying our modern civilizations.

THREE

GARLIC, THE GREAT HEALER

Garlic has great healing power, medical value and has a cure for what ails you. Garlic is a wonder food. Dr. Victor Gurewick, former director of Tufts University Vascular Laboratory at St. Elizabeth's University Hospital in Boston, Massachusetts in America conducted extensive tests on garlic and onions which showed their amazing ability to lower total cholesterol and protect against heart attacks and hardening of the arteries.

Garlic is used in Russia to kill bacteria and fight infections. Some tests indicate that garlic is more effective than antibiotics for specific types of bacterial infection. In Europe garlic is called "Russian penicillin." In the 1940's scientific investigation has proven that garlic acts as an antiseptic, fights infection and contains chemicals which prevent cancer. Garlic thins the blood, reducing clotting in high-risk heart patients, lowers the blood pressure, cholesterol, controls triglycerides, stimulates the immune system, prevents and relieves chronic bronchitis and acts as a decongestant and expectorant.

Garlic has an amazingly high sulfur content which makes all the difference. You should eat a clove or two a day. Cut up in salads and soups to enjoy its healing properties. Heart disease is the leading killer of Americans. Studies show garlic can reduce those numbers and protect you and your family.

"Garlic prevents heart attacks and strokes by controlling the key variables of high cholesterol, high triglycerides, high blood pressure and atherosclerosis, which is the deadly process of plaque formation and fat deposits inside the arteries. These factors create blockages in the circulatory system that can ultimately choke the blood flow to the heart muscle and brain," according to THE MIRACLE OF GARLIC AND VINEGAR book.

Kritchevsky's experiments demonstrated that rabbits fed on a diet that included garlic oil had 10% lower blood cholesterol levels and between 15 and 45 percent less fat in their arteries than rabbits that did not consume garlic oil. Studies confirmed that this effect held true for rats as well.

"The prestigious British Medical Journal, THE LANCET, published a study by two Indian cardiologists that showed that raw garlic will protect you from heart disease", according to the book THE MIRACLE OF GARLIC AND VINEGAR. The Indian cardiologists, Dr. Bordia and Dr. Bansal of the Department of Medicine at R.N.T. Medical College in Udaipur, India, found that garlic controls cholesterol so effectively that it even overcame the cardio-toxic effects of butter fat.

Dr. Martin Bailey of Georgetown University in Washington D.C. has produced laboratory evidence that adenosine, a chemical in garlic, blocks the production of fibronolytic, a compound in blood that makes blood sticky and causes clotting. "Adenonsine isn't the only weapon in garlic's arsenal" said chemistry professor Dr. Eric Block of the Albany Medical College. Dr. Block discovered ajoene, which is a medical marvel because it also has antibiotic qualities and promotes wound healing-garlic which can give untimely blood clots a knockout punch.

Dr. Block said that, "As an anti-athrombotic agent (clot buster), ajoene is as potent as aspirin." Aspirin has been recognized as one of the most effective anti-coagulants or blood thinners. Dr. Block's animal experiments show that a single dose of ajoene will shut down unwanted clotting by 100% and keep it away for 24 hours.

Studies indicate that garlic has no side effects of any kind. The only negative effect of garlic is the pungent odor. Dr. North conducted experiments showing garlic as a potent virus killer. Such diseases as polio, herpes and colds are cured by using garlic. Dr. North's data show garlic extract kills with nearly 100% effectiveness diseases such as human rhino-virus, which causes colds, para-influenza 3, a common flu and respiratory virus, herpes simplex 2, which is responsible for genital herpes. Garlic has killed polio virus with 90% effectiveness and has been proven to kill the deadly HIV virus. A concentrated pill with killing chemicals in garlic may be created soon. Dr. Michael Wargovich of the University of Texas, Anderson Hospital and Turner Institute , has found that mice treated with a chemical in garlic are 75% less likely to develop malignancies in the large bowel.

The National Cancer Institute is taking these findings seriously enough to investigate the matter and currently places garlic high on its list of chemo preventives which are substances that have the capacity to prevent carcinogens.

Dr. Lou demonstrated that garlic extract kyolic decreased this dead malignancy. Chinese researchers along with scientists at Cornell University and the National Cancer Institute, say that garlic as well as onions and scallions, can dramatically cut your risk of stomach cancer. You can triple your protection by eating more garlic, onions and scallions

The U.S. Department of Agriculture's Human Nutrition Center in Bettsville, M.D. has demonstrated that garlic can reduce levels of blood fat and blood sugar, too. Garlic increases the level of insulin in the blood. Therefore a person has better control over diabetes. Dr. Tarig Abdullah at Atbar Clinic and Research Institute in Panama City, Florida, produces dramatic evidence that garlic really revs up the boby's own, natural immune system. Dr. Abdullah and nine other volunteers ate either raw garlic or kyolic extract which are key immune system components such as white blood cells and killer cells (a type of white blood cell that attacks killer invaders). They were mixed in a lab dish with cancer cells.

The result was amazing. The killer cells from the garlic eaters destroyed 140% to 160% more cancer cells than did blood from non-garlic eaters. Abdullah believes that you can eat small doses of garlic and still be cured. He also believes that his findings may be of extreme importance to AIDS treatment. He claims he has not had a cold since he started eating a couple of cloves of garlic a day since 1973.

Garlic contains trace elements of germanium, selenium and alliance. In the 1940's Dr. Arthur Stoll, a Nobel, Prize-winning scientist discovered aliun, which is a germ fighting process. U.S. researchers stated that garlic is an effective defense against certain germs called gram negative organisms.

FOUR

89 YEAR OLD WOMAN HIKED ACROSS THE U.S.A.

Doris Haddock, who is 89 years old, has hiked around the U.S.A. She is from Dublin, New Hampshire. She walked thousands of miles to promote campaign finances reform in America. She later waged a quixotic campaign for the U.S. Senate. "Doris died at age 100", said Haddock spokeswoman Maude Salinger.

In 1999 and 2000, Haddock walked 3,200 miles to draw attention to campaign finance reform. In 2004, at age 94 she ran for the U.S Senate against Republican Judd Gregg. The subtitle of her autobiography written with Dennis Burke, was YOU'RE NEVER TOO OLD TO RAISE A LITTLE HELL!

"Doris Haddock's age wasn't a factor in what she did," Maude Salinger said. "She never gave up until the end. She advocated for public funding. She wanted people to know that democracy and government belong to us."

Doris Haddock became more active in community affairs after she retired. She was born on January 24, 1910 in Laconia, New Hampshire and attended Emerson College before marrying James Haddock. Doris Haddock worked at a shoe company for 120 years. She became interested in campaign finance reform after the defeat of Senator John McCain and Ruth Feingold, Democrat to remove unregulated "soft" money from campaigns in 1995. Then Haddock took a walking trip from Pasadena, California to Washington D.C.

In February, 2000, Doris Haddock said, "Sometimes I think it was a fool's errand, but I think there are more people in the country who know what campaign finance reform means which I started."

On New Year's Day in 1999 Haddock walked across more than 1,000 miles of desert, climbed the Appalachian Range in blizzard conditions and she even skied 100 miles after snowfall made roadside walking impossible.

When she made her way along California 62 near Twenty-nine Palms she marveled. She said, "The weather is divine. The mountains are a wonder, rising out of nowhere and the blue sky is always with you here."

In 2004, Doris Haddock entered the Senate race on the last day to file after the Democratic nominee dropped out when his campaign manager was accused of financial fraud. A few months before the election, Doris Haddock officially changed her name to "Granny D." She stressed that the "D" stood for Doris. However, she lost the election.

In her new book MY BOHEMIAN CENTURY Doris Haddock offers readers advice. "You have to keep the young adventurer inside your heart alive long enough for it to someday re-emerge. It may take some coaxing and some courage, but that person is in you always— never growing old."

It is very remarkable that Doris Haddock began campaigning at age 89. She proved that an older person can accomplish what younger people attempt to achieve. She was able to walk thousands of miles to communicate with different people. She slept outdoors and spent many hours outdoors in pleasant as well as severe weather, which is amazing for someone her age. She was determined to influence other people to promote democracy and to support honest, financial reform around America.

FIVE

HAND HELD GOOGLE TRANSLATOR

Google Translate can provide text translations in more than 50 languages. Google Inc. is using its vast computational and Intellectual resources to put the futuristic technology directly in the hands of consumers.

If you are in different places in the world, you can ask questions to find out how to locate what you want. For instance, "Where can I find a hamburger?" Moments later the phone will send out the phrase in different languages in a computerized voice.

You can ask someone who speaks a foreign language to speak into the phone. Wait a bit. Then press the play button to hear the translation." Is it going to rain today?" The phone's voice can sound like a robot from a 1950s era sci-fi movie and the translations are often less than perfect. Different people said the translating phrases work quite well.

"The free application called Google Translate, works on phones that run Google's Android operating system. It can translate text to and from more than 50 languages, including Icelandic, Slovenian and Swanhill, and has so far been downloaded more than 250,000 times since its January release," said David Sarno, journalist.

"There's still a long way to go, but this is an amazing start," said

Jaime Caarbonell, director of the Language technologies Institute at Carnegie Mellon University in Pittsburgh.

As of now, the only languages for which it recognizes spoken words are English, Mandarin and Japanese. German and several other languages are also included.

Google's founders realized early on in the company's 12 year history that if it was to achieve the goal of making the world's information easily accessible, its software would need to work in every language. We can break down the language barrier," said Franz Josef Och, who leads Google's machine translation group. He said that anyone can access any information or text on their independence of the language.

Och has a doctorate in Computer Science and was a machine translation researcher at USC before he began in 2004. He has written dozens of research papers on this subject.

Och stated that Arabic speakers are limited to 1% of Arabic texts Online. That limited amount of Arabic information greatly limits Arabic speakers in using Google in order to read a translated version of the Times Website.

In addition to the mobile application regular computer users can employ Google to translate entire Web pages. Google trains its computers to translate by constantly feeding them examples of a text that occurs in two or more languages. Many official United Nations documents are carefully translated into the languages of member countries.

Google's translation system can deduce the way many words and phrases are translated. The more examples it puts down, the smarter it gets.

"Google maintains an ever growing database containing text from billions of Web pages and periodicals and books in many languages. Its translator is not lacking for fodder," stated David Sarno.

"In recent years, Googles beefed up approach to translation has given it an advantage over most university research efforts," said Mark Przybocki, who oversees machine translation at the National Institute of Standards and Technology. NISTZ hosts an annual machine translation contest, but Google no longer participates. Pryybocki said, "Its competitors in the contest were going up against someone with access to a football field worth of processors to collect data." Przybocki said, "That's kind of not fair."

Google has high hopes for the mobile application even if it is in its early stages. Och believes that it won't be long until the technology will allow for speech-to-speech translation: that is, allowing for a live conversation between speakers of different languages.

Google has become a more universal, computer program for people to refer to in order to gather pertinent, worthwhile knowledge and information. Google offers a large amount of topics with available, valuable information that can be readily used for research.

SIX

NATURAL LIVING

Natural living is the best way to remain healthy physically, mentally and emotionally. Natural foods such as raw, organic fruits and vegetables, whole grains and nuts are the best to eat. Fresh air and plenty of sunshine are important to intake on a daily basis.

When you go walking outdoors in the woodlands and meadows you can absorb nature's ambiance. You are able to breathe in healing light and fragrances from many plants to keep you healthy. Appreciation of the natural beauty of nature will uplift and purify your body and mind.

People who live by Nature's laws are able to absorb healing forces regularly. Natural foods and water plus fresh, clean air help to heal your body and mind. Beautiful, colorful flowers, trees and scrubs will uplift you spiritually and emotionally.

Studies indicate that people who live naturally will generally live longer and have happier lives. Natural living promotes good health. It is very worthwhile to become close to nature. Closeness to nature generates a much better way of living.

Natural legumes, organic beans, fresh vegetables such as parsley, dark green lettuce, raw cabbage, organic carrots, cucumbers and tomatoes plus onions, garlic, celery and natural herbs such as thyme, oregano, basil, sea salt and garlic salt add enzymes and natural flavor to your food. Drink plenty of clean, spring water and herb teas such as chamomile, mint, lemon and Good Earth teas. Avoid man made and artificial foods and seasonings. Prepare mostly raw foods which are fresh. Drink organic fruit juices such as papaya juice, orange juice, apple juice, prune juice and pineapple juice. You will be much healthier and happier because you are living naturally.

SEVEN

SHIRLEY MACLAINE'S SPIRITUAL JOURNEY

"In these international bestsellers, OUT ON A LIMB and DANCING IN THE LIGHT and ALL IN THE PLAYING multitalented Shirley MacLaine described her own ongoing spiritual journey in search of harmony and self-transcendence. Now this celebrated actress, social activist and outspoken thinker shares an enlightened program of spiritual techniques and mental exercises to become healthier, happier and more attuned to the natural harmony of the world around and within ourselves," which is on the back cover of GOING WITHIN.

"In GOING WITHIN Shirley MacLaine answers many of the most challenging and important questions in seminars and interviews she has conducted from coast to coast," stated on the back cover of GOING WITHIN.

Shirley experienced transformations to seek inner peace and spiritual awareness. She was able to reach her highest potential in relationships at work and at home. She shows us how to reach a new level of love and harmony and reduce stress, overcome fear and to discover the joys of new and better ways of living.

Shirley MacLaine suggests that we use light, sound, crystals and visualizations to increase our personal energy. She said, "Explore the power of meditation to align body, mind and spirit." She continued,

"Understand and communicate with your hidden self-experience the stunning mysteries of psychic surgery and much more." Shirley MacLaine became aware of psychic phenomenon when she was searching for truth.

For seven years Shirley MacLaine had extraordinary adventures in Cosmic consciousness. She developed awareness, of her inner self by silencing her mind and meditating. Through spiritual technology her study took work, discipline and concentration. Shirley said, "To understand and love others begins with understanding and loving oneself. The more I applied the tools of what I investigated the more I found my own experience, my own attitudes and my own perceptions transforming my life into a more positive and peaceful adventure."

Shirley MacLaine believes millions of people all over the world are seeking to transform and improve their lives. She believes that answers for a changed world are not coming from sources outside of themselves. "The answers lie within," Shirley said.

GOING WITHIN offers keys for enlightening one's inner perceptions. Shirley MacLaine said, "It is a kind of personal roadmap for achieving spiritual clarity that can make the transformation an inner attitude improve outer reality." Shirley MacLaine traveled around the country attending seminars on inner transformation. She experienced an intense, face-to-face contact and sharing of deep, powerful and honest emotional struggles to help her articulate and shape her journey. She became more skilled in the techniques of meditation and visualization. She became aware of her body's esoteric centers of energy and their role in both physical and emotional healing.

Shirley MacLaine believes that we can find peace and bliss. Each of us can help leave a better world fit for our children to live in. It can become a world that is more trusting in the belief that inside each of us is a wealth of power to learn how to love and to be loved. Shirley MacLaine said, "The very urgency of the need for change will accelerate the metamorphosis required to proceed into the next century and the next millennium."

We can transform if we evaluate ourselves in how to overcome fear, doubt and human questioning. We can become one with our real self. When we experience unity, love, light and God reality we become aware of inner truths within. Shirley MacLaine has spoken and written about how to go within.

EIGHT

PREPARING GOURMET FOOD

Sandra Lee demonstrates how to prepare and cook many gourmet foods. She uses fresh food and some canned and packaged foods. She selects foods economically to save money. She has a food program on television. Within a half hour she prepares a full course meal each day from Monday through Friday.

Sandra Lee prepares the following gourmet meals. Pieces of chicken are washed. A flour mixture with eggs, salt, pepper, oregano canola oil is blended together. The flour mixture is placed in a plastic bag. Then pieces of uncooked chicken are placed in the plastic bag. Shake the plastic bag with the chicken to enfold each piece of chicken with the flour mixture. Put the chicken on a greased tray. Bake the chicken for one hour or more. Prepare pilaf rice by boiling water first. Pour wild rice into the boiling water. Chop up red and green peppers and celery. Pour them into the boiling rice. Let these vegetables simmer in the wild rice. Boil the rice for 20 to 30 minutes.

Sandra Lee prepared an organic salad with dark green lettuce, parsley scallions, garlic, carrots, celery and sliced tomatoes. Chop up all the ingredients mentioned. Mix all the chopped vegetables and add olive oil, thyme, and basil. Mix the salad again. Sprinkle parmesan cheese into the salad. Add salt and pepper into the salad.

Sandra Lee prepared dessert next. She planned to make apple pie in a skillet. She put three large chunks of butter into a skillet to melt.

She added one cup of brown sugar and half a cup of canola oil. She stirred the ingredients in the skillet. She added cinnamon for flavor. Sandra Lee prepared pie dough. She sifted whole wheat flour with canola oil and salt. She added one egg and mixed these ingredients. She added several tablespoons of baking soda to the dough. She pressed the mixture together to produce pie dough.

Sandra Lee opened a large can of sliced apples. She poured the canned, tart apples in a bowl. Meanwhile, she prepared fresh, raw, cut apples and mixed these apples with the tart canned apples. She added cinnamon and some water into the apples. After the apple mixture is mixed she added lemon juice and mixed it into the apples. She poured the cut apples into the skillet. She spread the apples in the skillet. Then she spread out the pie dough. She covered the apples and took off the edges around the skillet she sprinkled cinnamon on the pie dough. She cut openings. It was time to bake the apple pie for approximately 50 minutes at 35 degrees in the oven.

Sandra Lee prepared a delicious, cold drink. She placed ice in a blender. Then she added cherry juice, lemon juice and club soda and mixed these ingredients in the blender. Sandra poured this fruit drink in several glasses. When the entire dinner was ready, Sandra placed the chicken, rice pilaf, organic salad, apple pie and cold, fruit drinks on the table. Dinner was served.

NINE

GREAT MYSTERIES FROM THE ANCIENT WORLD

The Garden of Eden is described in THE BIBLE in the book of Genesis in the OLD TESTAMENT which was written language before Jesus Christ was living on Earth. The name "Eden: is linked to an Akkadian word meaning "a plain" or a Hebrew root meaning "delight" or "pleasant". From earliest times it was linked to the idea of Paradise. Old Persian apri-daeza means a park which became paradise in Hebrew and then paradeisos in Greek.

The most famous gardens are the Hanging Gardens of Babylon. These were one of the Seven Wonders of the ancient world. They were created by the Babylonian King Nebuchadnegger (604-562) for his Median wife, Amyitis, who pined for the wooded mountains of her native land. The image of the biblical Garden of Eden itself is of an earthly or a heavenly paradise to which human beings aspire as a place of rest." In Western civilization it relates to notions of a "Golden Age", the Happy Isles, the Islands of the Blessed and the Elysian fields", according to Brain M. Fagan, who edited THE SEVENTY GREAT MYSTERIES OF THE ANCIENT WORLD.

"In the BIBLE, Eden is a place of innocence, belonging in an age of innocence, when people could speak with God as with a friend. Today we are more ready to recognize that the Garden of Eden has its place only in our soul, where the meaning of a symbolic myth is more powerful then any concrete fact," said Brain M. Fagan. Who knows—the Garden of Eden could have been near the North Pole or in Africa. The climate could have changed considerably so that the Garden of Eden could have existed at the North Pole when it had a much warmer climate or in the Sahara Desert.

Another ancient mystery of the ancient world is the Biblical story of the Great Flood. Noah's Ark may have come to rest on the mountains of Ararat. Noah and his family survived the Great Flood. When the land dried out, Noah and his family left the wooden Ark. There were two of each animal that came off the Ark. Many expeditions have been made in search of Noah's Ark. One is Pir Omar Gydrun, called Mount Nisir, which lies near Kirkuk in Iraq (ancient Mesopotamia), east of the old Assyrian homeland in the Zagras Mountains. Another favored area is the Taurus Mountains east of Lake Von in Armenia. At the time of the Assyrian Empire (9th-17th centuries) this was the kingdom of Urartu. Mount Massius, the highest peak of this range, has been the object of expeditions to locate Noah's Ark.

"Someone called Deucalion, known as a Greek hero, had built an Ark. He loaded animals on board, set sail to avoid destruction. In ancient Mesopotamia the flood hero was at different periods called Ziusudra, Abrabasis and Ut-Napishtmim." It is this Mesopotamian legend that most closely resembles the story of Noah in the Hebrew Bible," said Brian M. Fagan. I believe Noah's Ark existed during Mesopotamia and that a large flood covered the Near East for a period of time. Noah and his family survived because they remained in a large, wooden Ark during a flood. I read that Noah's Ark was found in the mountains of Turkey in the 21st Century.

William Ryan and Walter Pitman, both geophysicists, think the Great Flood was a cataclysmic event which occurred in the Black Sea. There was a fresh water lake, called the New Euxine Lake by modern geologists at that time, its surface was 500 feet below sea level. The melting of glaciers at the end of the Ice Age had caused a rise in worldwide sea levels. An earthquake caused millions of gallons of salt water to flow into today's Bosporus and crashed eastwards through it, cascading down with immense violence into the lake far below. Flooding went on for a period of time.

The destruction of the city of Sodom and Gomorrah is one of the shocking stories told about in the Old Testament of the BIBLE. Lot went to live near Sodom, one of five prosperous cities of the plains of the Middle East of the Jordan valley. The men of Sodom were homosexuals. Lot was the only righteous person in Sodom. Two angels warned Lot of the impending destruction of Sodom. The Sodomites went to Lot's house in search of the angels. They blinded the Sodomites at the door. Then the angels told Lot to flee immediately with his family.

God rained down fire and brimstone on the cities of Sodom and Gomorrah. Lot and his family escaped towards the city of Zoar with their two daughters. Lot's wife disobeyed God's instructions when she looked back. She was turned into a pillar of salt. Lot and his two daughters survived. Natural erosion of the soft mounds around the Dead Sea produced pillars reminiscent of the fate of Lot's wife.

Another peculiar characteristic of the Dead Sea is that it is rich in bitumen, which surfaces as large lumps or oil slicks. The kings of Sodom and Gomorrah got stuck in slime pits as they fled during a battle with the kings of Syria.

Recent surveys and excavations along geological fault lines of the southern Dead Sea Basin conducted by Paul Lapp, Walter Rost, Thomas Shaub and Burton MacDonald in the 1970s and 1980s indicate that large, once thriving settlements existed. Bob edh-Drah ended with fiery destructions during the early Bronze Age 3000 B.C. In 1976, cities were found to be listed on Early Bronze Age tablets discovered at Elbla in Syria.

A church was uncovered over a cave in which early Byzantine Christians believed Lot took refuge after the destruction of Sodom and Gomorrah. The excavations at nearby sites have uncovered similar Middle Bronze Age artifacts. Physical evidence indicates that Sodom and Gomorrah really existed.

Atlantis was an ancient continent which existed 11,000 years ago. A first century A.D. marble sculpture of Plato (427-347 B.C) was the original source for the story of Atlantis. Plato introduced Atlantis and described its society in detail in two of his dialogues: *Timaeus* and *Critias*. *Critias* tells us that Atlantis was totally destroyed by the gods in a tremendous cataclysm of earthquakes and floods.

The Theosophists led by Helena Blavatsky suggested that Atlanteans flew in aeroplanes obtained from extraterrestrial aliens. Todney Castleden in his book, ATLANTIS DESTROYED, argues that Plato's Atlantis is a good match of a combination of Minoan Crete and Thera. "Plato's detailed description of Atlantis was intended necessarily to impress the reader with its material wealthy, technological sophistication and military power. What is more important is the way a people govern themselves. For Plato, the intellectual achievement of a perfect government and society is far more important, and is victorious over material, wealth, or power. In other words, it is more important how people are treated with kindness, fairness and compassion.

Jason and the Argonauts is another mystery of the ancient world. Jason was in search of new lands during ancient times. Jason agreed to set out on a quest. He had a seaworthy vessel constructed, the Argo and he acquired a crew of heroes and demigods, including Theseus, Hercules, and Orpheus to help him accomplish his task. After a challenging voyage through unknown waters, Jason and his Argonauts arrived in Colchis, where King Aeetes agreed to Jason's demand for the fleece after Jason goes through a series of trials. Jason was successful. He recovered the fleece and after an equally arduous voyage, he returned with the golden prize to his own kingdom.

Most scholars of Greek myths believe the kingdom of Colchis was located just as Apollonius described it, on the eastern margin of the Euxine Sea in the modern republic of Georgia. Historical and archaeological evidence shows that the Greeks explored and colonized the Black Sea's coast in antiquity. Greek colonies there date to the 8th century BC. The Argonauts sailed south where Apollonius understood that it flowed into the Mediterranean. The Argonauts then sailed south along the west coast of Italy, between the Wandering Rocks marking the straight between Sicily and , making landfalls on the North African Coast. Then he returned north and passed the eastern margin of Crete and finally arrived back in Iolus. Henriette Mertz in her book, THE WINE DARK SEA (1964) claims that Jason journeyed to Lake Titicaca, in Bolivia, South America. The Argonauts eventually sailed northward, parallel with the coast of North America, before returning home to Greece.

The ten lost tribes of Israel lived in 721 B.C. during the Assyrian King Sargon. The Great King marched south with his army through Syria and attacked the Israelites. The leader departed the leaders of Israel, together with their families to northern Syria to start new lives as farmers, craftsmen and traders. The people of Israel were the tribes of Reuben, God, Asher, Ephraim, Manossen, Don, Naphtali, Isschar, Simeon and Zebulon known as the ten Lost Tribes of Israel.

Orthodox Jews believe the twelve tribes still exist beyond the mythical River Sambatyon and that God will restore them to their homeland in the Messianic Age in accordance with biblical prophecy stated in Jermiah 31:7-8). Jews and Christians have searched for this fabled Jewish realm. Claims have been made by the Mormons, the Japanese, the Pathans of Pakistan, the Nepalese and the American Indians, as well as the British and Americans. The Book of Mormon claims that an angel gave Joseph Smith metal tablets from an ancient civilization that said one of the Lost Tribes migrated to North America and founded great cities. These were destroyed in a huge cataclysm and buried under mounds of Earth. The Mormons claim to base their beliefs on the Bible of this lost tribe in these tablets. The Mormon Bible reads much like a classical Bible. Yet, it adds many other prophets and writers from this lost tribe. Only in recent years have ruins and artifacts been discovered from this lost civilization. Details and photos are in books by Frank Joseph, available in Barnes and Nobles and Borders.

"Jews migrated eastward and westward to Arabia and China and possibly to India. The Pathans are devoted Moslems who live in Pakistan, India, Afghanistan and Iran. They also call themselves Beni Israel (People of Israel). They have maintained many Jewish customs such as the Sabbath. The Mizo tribe and the Beni Menaske (Children of Manasseh) in Burma worship Y'wa, which means God of Israel. And in northwest China there are people called the Ciiang-min who believe they are descendants of Abraham. They have a special priestly caste who offer sacrifice and place emphasis on ritual purity", stated Brian M. Fagan. Jews have migrated to many locations such as to Russia, throughout Europe and to America as well. They were treated like outcasts in Germany before World War 2. They took over Palestine. This has caused problems with the people of Palestine for many centuries.

"The Lemba tribe may have the DNA marker found in Jewish men. The senior Lemba clan, the Bhuba, show a very much higher incidence of this chromosome marker—as high as 53.8 per cent, which is approaching the rate among the Jewish Cohanim themselves. We may be able to find the families of some lost Jews of the past two millennia," stated Brian M. Fagan. There may be other African tribes with Jewish DNA. Jews may have intermarried with other tribes.

The Ark of the Covenant is another mystery in ancient times. The Ark of the Covenant was traditionally carried into battle by marching around Jericho, helping the Israelites to capture them during their conquest of the Promised Land. Many people believe that the Ark was destroyed when the Babylonians captured and devastated Jerusalem in 587/6 BC. Some Rabbis believed that the prophet Jeremiah had concealed the Ark on Mount Nebas. Others thought that King Josiah (639-609 BC) had hidden the Ark in a deep cave right on the Temple Mount below the Holy of Holies of the temple.

Old Arab chronicles report that the Ark was taken to safety in Arabia. There is a belief that the Ark is concealed in the vaults of the Vatican. Some believe the Ark was captured by the Egyptian Pharaoh Shitake when he raided deep into Canaan. Another theory is that the Romans burned down the Second Temple in AD 70 and the Ark was rescued via underground tunnels that led eastwards over 30km (19 miles) to the neighborhood of Qumran where it still lies buried. Some people believe the Ark was stolen and taken to Ethiopia by Menelek, son of King Solomon and the Queen of Sheba. The Ethiopian Church claims the Ark of the Covenant is concealed among them.

The Ark of the Covenant was made of acacia wood and lined inside and outside with pure gold. It has a solid gold cover or lid with two cherubim whose wings protect the Ark. The sacred teachings given to Moses are stored inside the Ark of the Covenant.

TEN

THE SPECTACULAR GARDEN

Cecelia Pace loved viewing spectacular gardens. She made a hobby of gardening. She selected a variety of annual and perennial flowers to plant in her country estate gardens. She attended garden parties as often as she could to enjoy the magnificent beauty and fragrance of each garden.

Cecelia came to a spectacular garden one day which was more remarkable than any garden she had seen before. This spectacular garden was in Florida near the Everglades. Many tropical flowers were blooming everywhere such as orchids, Birds of Paradise, pansies and lilies. There were at least twenty types of orchids growing in this spectacular garden.

Tropical trees such as palm trees, fan trees and Norfolk Pines were growing abundantly throughout this splendid garden. There were at least 30 acres with a variety of plants. Cecelia wandered up and down different pathways. She came to a large pond where there were frogs sitting on large, green lily pads. Some of the frogs were croaking. They expanded their throats before they croaked. Some frogs leaped across the pond. Some frogs sunned themselves on the lily pads. Some frogs jumped from one lily pad to another lily pad. Gold fish and carps were swimming in the pond. Cecelia looked carefully in the pond. The water was around fifteen feet deep. Plants were growing in the pond. Cecelia was fascinated with fireflies which were flying by. They lit up. Polliwogs were moving in the pond.

Some flamingos were walking by at the pond. They had landed there to find food in the pond as well as to rest in the sun. Their long necks and pink feathers were interesting to observe. There were at least two dozen flamingos flocking together at the pond. They looked majestic as they moved around.

Cecelia walked near the edge of the pond. She saw ducks and some geese gliding in the water. They were following the lead duck and goose in a southern direction in the pond. It was a warm, tropical day.

Cecelia decided to sit near the pond. The water currents were moving. Ducks and geese scooped down to catch insects in the pond with their beaks. Cecelia watched how the ducks, geese and frogs behaved in the pond as she sat there relaxing. She felt at peace in this magnificent setting. She sat there for awhile to rest.

After a while Cecelia stood up and continued walking through the gardens. She came to roses which were growing in rose bushes. There were white, red, pink and purple. Many roses were blooming in clusters as she walked down pathways. She smelled the fragrances of the colorful roses. Cecelia continued to walk through this spectacular garden. She stopped to look at trees covered with vines on their trunks. She was amazed at the designs of clustered vines on the trees.

As Cecelia continued to walk she observed colorful, tropical birds in different trees. Some were parrots. Others were parakeets. Cockados had large pointed beaks. They were eating seeds and nuts with their long beaks. Cecelia watched the tropical birds in this extraordinary garden. The sun began to move lower in the west. Beautiful colors emerged in the sky.

A sunset was forming in the sky. Cecelia realized it was late afternoon. She walked back to the entrance of the garden. She sat on a garden bench and observed a brilliant, crimson sunset. She observed orange, yellow, red, pink and lavender colors in the sky. This sunset was very magnificent

Cecelia walked to her car after observing the sunset. She drove back to her motel to rest for the night. She thought about her marvelous experience at the spectacular garden. She planned to go back to this extraordinary garden someday.

ELEVEN

BOOKS, BOOKS
AND MORE BOOKS

Books have been printed for many centuries. There are many valuable books in the world. There are at least seven, ancient BIBLES which describe historical happenings and important events. Early prophets and sages have recorded philosophical and religious truths in ancient BIBLES.

Religious laws and prophecies have been recorded in ancient BIBLES. Inner truths such as reincarnation mean we are reborn again and again in different embodiments to learn what we can on Earth. Karma (cause and effect) is mentioned in ancient BIBLES. Laws of Nature are described in ancient BIBLES in different languages such as Arabic, Egyptian, Sumerian, Babylonian, etc.

Egyptians wrote books on papyrus paper with feathered pens. The papyrus was rolled up and kept in shelves. These papyrus documents contained important knowledge which the Egyptian scholars recorded in the Egyptian written language.

There are classics stored in public and private libraries. Children's stories, historical accounts and documents are in volumes of books written by scholars around the world. Many great writers such as Plato, Socrates, Leonardo Da Vinci, Lord Byron, Lord Tennyson, Ralph Waldo Emerson, Henry Wadsworth Longfellow, Robert Frost, Shakespeare,

Emily Barrett Browning, Ernest Hemingway and many other writers have had classics published.

Many enrichment books are available in libraries and book stores. Thousands of books have been written and published. There are reference books, encyclopedias, journals, biographies, autobiographies, poetry, short stories, fables, novels, cartoons and educational books.

Books are valuable. Books, books and more books are available in book stores, public and private libraries, schools and book stands. Books are important to read.

TWELVE

ABOUT THE SECRET DOCTRINE

THE SECRET DOCTRINE is a valuable, theosophical book written by Madame Helena Blavatsky from Russia in 1888 through 1991. THE SECRET DOCTRINE is a thick book, of over 550 pages. It is an esoteric doctrine for the higher members of the Occult Brotherhoods. "It contains, she says, just as much as can be received by the world during this coming century."

"The World she explains means Man living in the Personal Nature. The "world" will find in the two volumes of THE SECRET DOCTRINE all its utmost comprehension which can be grasped." Every form, no matter how crude, contains the image of its "creator" concealed within it. So, likewise does an author conceal information.

"There is neither coming nor passing, but eternal becoming, Madame Blavatsky said. The first thing to do, even if it takes years, is to get some grasp of the "Three Fundamental Principles" given in the Proem. Follow that up by study of the Recapitulation—the numbered items in the Summing up to Volume 1, Part 1. Then take the preliminary notes (Volume 2) and the Conclusion (Vol. 3)."

H.P.B. seems pretty definite about the importance of the teaching (in the Conclusion) relating to the times of coming of the Races and Sub-races. The Fourth Root-race is still alive. So are the third, second and first. Their manifestations on our present planet of substance are present. The Sixth Sub-Race is also here. "Disciples and Brothers as well as Adepts can't be people of the everyday Fifth Sub-Race, for the race is a state of evolution.

The New Race had dawned definitely on the World. According to her the duration of a Sub-Race for humanity at large coincides with that of the Sidereal Year (the circle of the Earth's axis—about 25,000-26,000 years).

Madame Helena Blavatsky stated that fundamental unity is important. Fundamentally there is One Being. This Being has two aspects, positive and negative. The positive is Spirit or Consciousness. The negative is substance, the subject of consciousness. This Being is the Absolute in its, primary manifestation. There is nothing outside of being absolute. It is all Being. It is clear that this fundamental One Existence, or Absolute Being, must be the Reality in every form there is.

"The Atom, the Man, the God (she said) are each separately as well as all collectively, Absolute Being in their last analysis; that is their real individuality. Every last atom is alive. It cannot be otherwise, since every atom of substance, no matter of what plane, in itself is a life.

"Theosophy is for those who can think or for those who can drive themselves to think not as mental sluggards," said Helena Blavatsky, who had established the Theosophical Society in 1875. She said there is no dead matter. All the Hierarchies of the Heavens exist within him. She stated that truth is neither Macrocosm nor Microcosm but One Existence. Great and small are such only as viewed by a limited consciousness." In other words, all life is part of One Great Reality. We exist in seven planes of awareness and consciousness. Life continues to evolve and change.

The fourth and last basic idea is that the great Hermatic Axiom sums up and synthesizes all the others. "As is the inner, so is the outer. As is the great, so is the small; as is above, so it is below; there is but One Life and Law and he that worketh it is One. Nothing is inner; nothing is outer; nothing is high, nothing is low, in the Divine Economy."

Helena Blavatsky said, "The brain is the instrument of working consciousness and every conscious mental picture formed means change and destruction of the brain. Ordinary intellectual activity moves on well beaten paths in the brain and does not compel sudden adjustments and destructions in its substance. This new kind of mental effort calls for the carving out of new "brain paths", the ranking in different order of the little brain lives. This mode of thinking is what the Indians call Janana Yoga. Mental images eventually form into mental pictures. The new mental picture may not relate to reality. Images may become dull and are discarded. New mental images may be more beautiful than the last ones. Even the last picture will fade like the others". Madame Blavatsky said, "The process goes on until at last the mind and its pictures are transcended and the learner enters and dwells in the world of no form, but of which forms become formless. Reflections are images which disappear."

"The true student of THE SECRET DOCTRINE is a Janana Yogi and this Path of Yoga is the True Path for the Western student," said Robert Bowen, Commander of R.N. Yoga is the key to God realization and higher consciousness. When a soul goes within to seek spiritual truth, inner wisdom is revealed.

THIRTEEN
AMAZING WONDERS

Amazing wonders exist in the world in our solar system and our Universe. For instance, light, heat, motion, magnetism, electromagnetism, Cosmic forces of positive and negative energy exist which help keep balance and equilibrium on our planet in the solar system and the Universe.

Fohat is cosmic energy which is interpenetrated within all life. Life forms are created by the Sons of Fohat. Each physical life substance has an astral form within it which is invisible. The astral form is a duplicate of the physical form on another invisible plane. Life forms begin on the astral plane before they descend to the physical plane.

It is amazing how life forms are created. Each life form has a Blue Print with the creative plan recorded in it. Human beings slowly grow in the mother's womb over nine months. The human fetus continues to grow step by step. When a baby is born he or she has a DNA factor determines what sex he or she is. The DNA factor determines what sex he or she is. The DNA determines the color of the baby's eyes, skin and hair. Generally a boy looks like its mother and a girl looks like her father. The height of the baby is determined by its blueprint. Fingernails and toe nails grow before birth. Hair and eyelashes grow while the baby is in the womb. Step by step the baby grows inside the womb. It is amazing how each organ of the human body develops.

A human fetus develops from a very tiny substance continuing the entire human plan. It is amazing how a microscopic creation forms into a macrocosm which is a much larger form. Substances are formed by the creator. Billions of cells form within each organ of the body. The human body is an amazing creation with many organs and functions. The human brain has different sections which control the body because of its intelligence. The human mind is capable of thinking with intelligence. This is an amazing phenomenon.

The ecosystem in Nature is amazing. Each creature helps to keep a balance. Survival of the fittest exists in Nature. Each living thing learns to survive. The four elements of fire, air, water and earth effects life in Nature. There must be enough oxygen, water and food from plants and animals so creatures can survive.

Birth of each creature is an amazing experience. There is a certain time each new born creature comes into the world. Each creature has a life cycle. Some animals live much longer than other animals. Each animal eats certain foods. Some animals only eat vegetables and fruits. Other animals eat meat. Life goes on and on.

Some animals have lived for millions of years on Earth. Their species have learned to adapt and survive over a long period of time. They have survived despite severe earthquakes, extreme climates, floods and other disasters. This is amazing in itself.

The Earth moves in a specific motion around the Sun. The planets are spaced apart far enough from one another as they all orbit around the Sun. What is most amazing is that there are millions of solar systems in our Universe. Different solar systems exist in different galaxies in the Universe. There is life everywhere in the Universe. Life forms may be very different on each planet. We will be amazed to learn about life forms on other planets because they are very different than we are in how they function and survive. They may exist without oxygen and even water.

Amazing wonders are taking place every day. We need to be aware of new life forms on our planet, Earth. We should be open-minded about what we observe in the ocean, in remote places and unusual locations. Many plants and some unknown animals are yet to be discovered, observed and given names. It is amazing how certain life forms exist in the deepest parts of the vast ocean.

Amazing wonders exist on other planets in our solar system. The inner planets are closest to the Sun. Life can exist underground on Venus and Mars where temperatures are very different and water can be found. Life can exist definitely on Earth. Each life form is unique which is amazing. Multiple cells exist with many functions in order to promote life substance and energy.

FOURTEEN

THE AMETHYST STONES

Amethyst stones are purple or violet quartz with shining clusters in larger stones. Pisces wear the amethyst stone which represents Pisces birthstone. Amethyst stones are spiritual symbols. They are displayed in churches, museums and art galleries. Amethyst stones are sold in jewelry stores.

Amy Beecham was a Pisces which was her birth sign. She went to a jewelry store in New York City to look for an amethyst stone to display in her home. She took a bus to Fifth Avenue downtown New York City. She went to Tiffany's first to look at amethyst stones. She walked into this expensive jewelry store. Jewelry was displayed under glass inside jewelry, display tables.

There were pearl necklaces, pearl rings, diamond bracelets, diamond necklaces and diamond rings. Finally, Amy saw some amethyst stones, amethyst rings and larger amethyst stones which were four feet tall. They were on platforms being displayed around the room. Amy enjoyed looking at the amethyst stones. She noticed the prices of the amethyst stones were very expensive. Amy didn't have enough money to pay for any of the amethyst stones.

Amy decided to leave Tiffany's. She walked around downtown to browse in other jewelry stores. Finally, she came to a jewelry store where the jewelry was much less expensive. She looked around carefully for amethyst stones. She saw a beautiful, amethyst ring which was $29.99.

She tried this ring on. It fit just right. Amy decided to buy the amethyst ring. She wrote a check for the total amount which was the price plus the tax.

The amethyst ring looked very attractive on Amy's finger. She was wearing her birthstone. Amy left the jewelry shop. She was happy because she had purchased an amethyst ring. Violet and purple were Amy's favorite colors. She planned to wear her new ring regularly. Amy hoped to purchase more amethyst stones in the future.

FIFTEEN

THE PARANORMAL TRAVELS OF MARK TWAIN

Mark Twain, a well known American writer, began by working in a printing shop and newspaper. He learned to write newspaper articles first. In time, he began writing short stories and poems. His real name was Samuel Clemens. He wrote THE ADVENTURES OF HUCKLEBERRY FINN in 1884-1885.

Mark Twain had a precognitive dream about his brother Henry. He dreamt that his brother had died and that he was in a casket. The casket was sitting on some chairs. Mark Twain, known as Samuel Clemens, wrenched himself out of sleep. He felt grief because his dream seemed so real. Samuel Clements's brother Henry went on a ship, The Pennsylvania several days later. Sam went on another steamboat called Lacey.

Two days later the Lacey's crew and passengers heard a shout from the shore. "The Pennsylvania was a blown up ship and a hundred and fifty lives were lost." A boiler had exploded, destroying the steamboat. Passengers had been blown into the river, "boiled alive, decapitated, impaled." Sam found out that his brother, Henry had been "hurt beyond help."

When Lacey arrived at Memphis, Samuel Clements rushed to the hospital where his brother laid injured. Henry had been sleeping above the boilers. He was blown into the air, dropped back on the heated boilers and bombarded by falling debris. Henry lived for three days. He finally died. Henry's casket was laid on two wooden chairs just like he saw in his dream.

Samuel Clements, known as Mark Twain, had many brushes with the supernatural during his life, but none as spectacular as this. "The Missouri born writer, who would become known as the "American Altair," got used to rubbing shoulders with the beyond. He developed a theory to explain the mechanics of these psychic encounters. He had a second "spiritual" or "dream" self.

We have seven bodies. We have a mental body, emotional body, an astral body and a physical body. Our astral body is within our physical body. We are capable of experiencing extrasensory perception. Paranormal experiences can occur in our dreams. We have an inner eye and inner ear which we use frequently. Messages may be sent to us so that we find out information from the astral plane.

SIXTEEN

BE YOURSELF

Learn to be yourself. Too often a person imitates the behavior of other people. To be oneself means to behave naturally. You should respond in a natural manner. To show off and behave like someone else means a person prefers to be like someone else. You need to believe and have faith in yourself.

Self confidence should be developed during childhood and young adulthood. To know oneself is the way to self realization and awareness. Spiritual awakening leads to enlightenment and illumination. To know the Real Self is the way to soul fulfillment. So, be your Real Self in order to become aware of who you really are. Become One with All life. You will be appreciated more when you are yourself.

FICTION

SEVENTEEN

HARMONIOUS TIMES

Harmonious times help a person to be happy, well adjusted and in tune with life. When we feel at peace and we have positive relationships with others we feel better about ourselves. Effective communications and positive feelings help us feel harmonious.

Alice Starr was a vivacious, enthusiastic individual. She reached out to her family, friends and new acquaintances. Alice tried to maintain a pleasant relationship with everyone she came in contact with. She was cheerful and eager to communicate with her family members, friends and new acquaintances.

Alice decided to invite her friends to a slumber party at her home. Her mother said it was alright for Alice to have a slumber party. Alice was happy because she would be able to enjoy visiting and having fun with her friends. She called eleven of her girl friends to bring their bedrolls and pillow to her house on Saturday at 5 p.m. in two weeks on June 14th.

Mrs. Starr, Alice's mother, helped Alice prepare food for Alice's friends to enjoy such as hot dogs with relish, mustard, catsup on long buns with roasted wieners, potato chips, jello, cookies, hamburgers and ice cream. When Alice's friends arrived on June 14th, they brought their bedrolls and pillows. The girls sat around in the living room of Alice's home. They told stories and jokes and laughed a lot. The girls were having a good time at the slumber party.

Alice and her mother brought food into the living room to a big table. Alice and her friends enjoyed eating hot dogs, hamburgers, potato chips, sliced, raw vegetables such as baby tomatoes, carrots and cucumbers. After they ate these foods they were served ice cram and cookies plus fruit punch.

After the girls finished eating they lay down on their bedrolls to visit. Then they sang some folk songs and school songs. Then some of the girls decided to demonstrate stunts and roles while the other girls tried to guess who they were pretending to be. Everyone had a good time. Alice was having a wonderful time with her friends.

The next morning after the twelve girls had breakfast, they played games such as scrabble, chess, checkers and monopoly. The girls went home after lunch. They all had a good time.

Alice went to the beach with two of her friends. They went swimming in the ocean. Then they decided to lie on towels on the beach to sun themselves and to dry off. Alice and her friends went for a long walk on the beach. They gathered shells in the sand.

The girls watched the sunset in the late afternoon. The bright colors were scintillating. The sun went down over the horizon gradually. Bright hues of orange, yellow, violet and some white streaks were visible in the sky over the ocean. The girls watched the sunset for at least an hour.

Alice and her friends eventually went home. It was Sunday evening. They would be going to school the next day. Alice thought about the fun she had during the weekend with her friends. She was glad to have a harmonious time.

EIGHTEEN

WHY WE SHOULD KEEP ALERT

Keeping alert is important so that we can become aware of our environment. Many things are occurring and taking place all the time.

Birds fly around and perch in trees, on shrubs and on the ground. The Sun shines on shrubs and on the ground. The Sun moves across the sky everyday. Butterflies flutter around near trees and bushes. Butterflies have bright colors. They flutter their wings as they move around. Observe how squirrels scurry up tree trunks into branches. Their bushy tails are interesting to look at especially when they are moving about.

Be alert when you walk through a forest. Many plants grow such as sword ferns, lichen, mosses and grass. Wild hares jump about and hide in the grass and bushes. We should be alert regarding insects such as spiders, flies, mosquitoes and gnats. Forests may have deer roaming around. Many forests have brown and black bears wandering around in forest valleys and mountainsides. Bears can be dangerous. People need to be on guard in the wilderness. Bears tend to attack animals and people. Deer roam around. Many forests have brown and black bears wandering around in forest valleys and mountainsides. Bears can be dangerous. People need to be on guard in the wilderness. Bears tend to attack animals and people.

We should be alert to avoid other dangers such as old bridges which are capable of falling apart. During heavy rain it may flood. Avoid driving and walking during floods. Try to evacuate the area where the flood is taking place.

Avoid driving a tractor unless you remain alert and careful all of the time. Have your car lights and blinkers checked for mechanical failures regularly. Be sure your car lights and blinkers are working. Be alert at all times when you drive a car. Check that you are in the correct gear. Be sure your car brakes are working correctly.

Being alert may save your life during unexpected problems and dangers. Being alert keeps you younger and healthier.

NINETEEN

RARE MOMENTS

Rare moments come and go. Sometimes we have unusual experiences. We can recall rare moments in our lives. Very special moments are worth remembering.

Attending school dances may be very memorable. This is an opportunity to meet the opposite sex. Girls are able to meet guys who ask them to dance. A gal may meet someone special at a dance. The memory of dancing with someone who is attractive and interesting can take place at a dance.

Social clubs and activities are places to meet more interesting people. There are chess clubs, foreign language clubs, home economics clubs, writing clubs, sports clubs, Social Science and UFO clubs. It is meaningful to meet other people who have common interests and hobbies. Book clubs are very worthwhile places to meet other people who like to read.

Sally Weathers liked to read. She went to bookstores to buy current books. While she was browsing through different, interesting books, a fellow with blonde hair, blue eyes and a slender form, came to browse at books close by. He kept looking at books. Sally had selected a UFO book from the shelf to look at closely.

The fellow, whose name was Alex, spoke to Sally. He said, "The UFO book you are looking at is the book I have been searching for. May I look at this book?" Sally handed the book to Alex. The title was

ALIEN ENCOUNTERS. Alex thumbed through this book carefully. Then Alex said, "I hope you will let me have this book. I have been studying about UFOs and aliens."

Sally looked at Alex warmly and said, "Sure. You can take this book. I can order this book. I don't see a second copy." Alex smiled and said, "Thanks for letting me purchase this book." Sally replied, "How long have you been interested in UFOs and aliens from other planets?" Alex replied, "I have studied UFOs and aliens for many years. I have done a thorough investigation about life on other planets."

Sally asked, "When did you see UFOs?" Alex replied, "Recently, I saw a silver saucer shaped UFO hovering near where I live. It stopped in the sky for awhile. Then it disappeared very quickly" Sally looked interested in what Alex told her. She asked, "Have you ever seen any UFOs land on Earth?" Alex answered, "I saw a small, round UFO land on the ground. It was too far away so I didn't have enough time to approach it. It sped away quickly after five minutes."

Sally was fascinated with Alex's encounters with UFOs. Alex said, "I attend a UFO group once a week. Would you like to come to the UFO group?" Sally replied, "Yes. When do you meet?" Alex replied, "We meet on Wednesday night from 7 a.m. to 9 p.m. at the Recreation Center in town." Sally looked excited and appeared enthusiastic about attending the UFO group. Alex said, "I will pick you up around 6:45 p.m. and bring you to the UFO group." Sally replied, "Wonderful. I would like to go this Wednesday night." Alex smiled and said, "Where do you live?" Sally gave Alex her address and phone number.

Alex and Sally purchased several books at the bookstore. Then Sally and Alex left the bookstore to go about doing other activities. Sally went shopping for a new clothing outfit. She stepped into a dress shop down the street. Sally tried on different pant suits which were green, violet, yellow and salmon colored. Sally selected a violet suit with a yellow scarf to tie around her neck. She also bought a green blouse to match her violet pant suit.

Sally went further down the street until she came to a beauty parlor. She walked into the beauty saloon and had her hair cut and styled. She went home with her new pant suit. When she got home she heard the phone ringing as she walked in the door. Sally answered the phone. Alex was on the phone. He said, "Hi. This is Alex. I would like to take you out to dinner." Sally responded, "Great. When?" Alex replied, "How about tonight?" Sally replied, "Sure." Alex said, "I will pick you up at 6:30 p.m. You live at 240 Elm St. Is this the correct address?" "Yes. Go down Marsh Street and turn right on Elm Street. My house is green with a gold rimming. It is the fourth house on the right hand of the street. I will be ready at 6:30 p.m." "Alex spoke, "I will be there. See you later." Both of them hung up after saying goodbye.

That night Sally wore her new, violet, pant suit with the new, green blouse and yellow neck scarf. Her red hair was curly and stylish. She looked very attractive. She was twenty-five years old. Alex arrived at 6:30 p.m. as planned. Sally greeted him at the front door. He took her to his four door sedan Nissan car. He opened the front passenger door for Sally. She stepped into his car. She noticed how clean his car looked inside as well as outside.

Alex said, "Do you like seafood?" Sally replied, "I love seafood." Alex said, "I am taking you to a well known seafood restaurant at the wharf. The food is excellent there." Alex started the engine of his car. He drove to the wharf near the ocean. He came to Pete's Seafood Restaurant. Alex and Sally walked into this restaurant after the car was parked. The host seated Alex and Sally at a table near a window view.

The window view was spectacular at the restaurant. The ocean view was interesting. Alex and Sally gazed at the deep, blue ocean. Waves were splashing on the beach. A brilliant sunset was spread across the sky. Alex and Sally looked at a menu. Alex decided to order salmon with rice pilaf and a medley of vegetables. He also ordered clam chowder. Sally ordered seabass, scalloped potatoes and a green salad. She also ordered clam chowder. They both ordered herb tea.

Alex looked at Sally warmly. He said, "I'm glad I met you. I have a lot to tell you about my experiences with UFOs and beings from outer space." Sally looked at Alex with interest. He continued by saying, "I have met some beings from Orion and the Pleiades." Sally eagerly asked, "What do they look like?" Alex replied, "The Pleiadeans I saw were tall with blonde hair and red hair. They had purple-blue eyes and white skin. They wore white and purple robes and sparkling sandals."

Sally asked, "Were the Pleiadeans friendly?" Alex answered, "They were both friendly and capable of communicating intelligently. I learned a lot from them about our solar system and our galaxy." Sally responded, "How fascinating. I wish I could meet the Pleiadeans." Alex replied, "Perhaps you will meet them someday." Sally looked at Alex with a gleam in her eyes.

The server brought the soup. Alex and Sally began eating their clam chowder. Alex put crackers in his soup. Then the main course was served. There were whole wheat rolls and butter on the table. Sally selected a roll. She split it in half and she buttered each half of the roll. Sally enjoyed eating the buttered roll with her soup.

Alex continued speaking as he ate his sumptuous, salmon dinner. He said, "The Orions are called the Grays. They have large eyes, tiny noses, mouths and large heads. They have frail bodies and long hands and fingers." Sally asked, "How did they behave?" Alex answered, "The Grays appeared emotionless. They were not warm and friendly. They appeared to be robots. I didn't respond to them because they were cold."

Alex and Sally continued to eat their dinner. They listened to relaxing, dinner music while they enjoyed their fish dinner. Sally thought about what Alex told her about The Pleiadeans and the Grays. She didn't want to meet the Grays. After dinner, Alex and Sandy were served strawberry ice-cream with fresh strawberries on top with chocolate syrup poured over the ice-cream for dessert.

Sally thanked Alex for treating her to dinner. Alex paid for the meal. Alex and Sally left the restaurant and they walked on the beach to look at the stars and moon. Alex pointed out different constellations such as The Big Dipper, Little Dipper, Orion and the Pleiades. They continued to walk on the beach as they gazed at the night sky. Sally hoped to see some UFOs. However, no UFOs were visible that night.

When Wednesday night came Alex picked Sally up to go to the UFO group. Sally met people at this UFO group who were also interested in UFOs and aliens from other planets. She listened to different people in the group talk about their experiences with UFOs and outer space beings. Sally kept learning about outer space beings and UFOs. She continued to attend this group for years to come. These UFO meeting were enlightening and worthwhile. Sally became good friends with Alex over a period of years. She hoped to witness UFOs in the sky and on the ground as well as beings from outer space.

NONFICTION

TWENTY
SPLENDID OCCURRENCES

We enjoy splendid times and we want to repeat pleasant experiences as often as we can. We enjoy sunny, warm days and special occasions. Many people like to sing, dance and attend celebrations in the community.

Harvest Festival is a good time to celebrate Autumn. People dress up in costumes. Some people participate in parades. Other people work at booths downtown, old Arroyo Grande. They enjoy eating hot dogs, hamburgers, French fries, potato salad, snow cones, apple pie, donuts, cookies, ice cream, cotton candy and fast food Chinese food.

The Harvest Festival parade is very festive. The Gay Nineties costumes are colorful and have a distinct style. Women wear long skirts with high neck blouses and long dresses. Men wear special, rimmed hats and suits with vests. Flowers are arrayed along the main street where the parade takes place. Different floats are displayed in the parade which depicts Autumn themes and Gay Nineties topics. Girls in Mexican skirts and sombrero hats dance in the streets. This occurs from year to year. Harvest Festival occurs once a year. This festival is special and splendid.

Rainbows occur from time to time in the sky while it rains and after it stops raining. Beautiful, reflecting hues of color arch together in a half circle. You can see red, yellow, green, orange and sometimes violet colors. It is a splendid occurrence to witness rainbows.

Sunset occurs in the early evening. Sunsets occur regularly on clear nights. Brilliant colors of red, orange, yellow, violet and sometimes light purple can be seen at the edge of the horizon. Sunsets reoccur regularly and they are wonderful to observe.

Raindrops sparkle on leaves, grass and on pine needles after it has rained. Raindrops dazzle in the light. Their reoccurring sparkles are fascinating to observe again and again.

TWENTY-ONE

NEW AGE EDUCATION

New Age education is very important. Many age groups should be learning to awaken to higher consciousness. Learning how to become aware of the Real Self and higher mind is vital to the growth of the soul.

Children as well as adults should be learning about the inner centers or charkas, inner eye center, heart center, solar plexus center and lower spine center. The inner centers exist and each charka affects the soul. The crown charka is a starry paint in the upper half of one's head. The inner eye is between the two eyes. Astral images are seen in the inner eye. Love and light flows through the heart center. The emotions are stored in the solar plexus. The lower spine charka contains the caduceus fires.

New Age education should enlighten the soul and awaken one's consciousness to inner truths, laws of life and awareness of God reality and God consciousness.

We have the opportunity to learn about our purpose for incarnating on Earth. We should learn about spiritual phenomenon. We need to become aware of outer space and inner space. We should become aware of Nature and how the fire elementals and air elementals function and work on Earth.

Children should learn about soul realization and God realization at an early age so they can perceive their environment as well as the world in general with more awareness. Children and adults should become aware of the seven planes of existence. We have a mental, emotional, physical and invisible, astral body.

Understanding who we are plus learning to relate to others is very important. We will understand the world we live in much better by becoming One with all life as we grow and learn about life.

Inner space travel is even more important than outer space travel. Learning about inter-dimensions helps us expand our awareness of creation. Matter, force and consciousness are interconnected. Life on the matter plane depends on the support of the invisible, astral plane. There are parallel planes in which astral life exists. Inter-dimensions function to protect the outer plane. The physical plane is the densest. Matter molecules move much slower than creations on the astral plane.

Our God presence is stored with knowledge of our Earth and the Cosmic plan. We need to learn to go within to become aware of the realities of God creation in order to become truly educated. New Age education is an ongoing experience. True enlightenment is experienced by those souls who have become One with the true realities of life.

An experimental "Planetary Civilization", based on the equality and unity of humanity is called "The Xians." In the 1970s the Xians successfully created the type of educational system described in this chapter. The Xians used their Cosmic University, Maui Free University, The Floating Cosmic University yacht, The Solar Energy University and The Future Age Center's Department of Enlightenment, to manifest this curriculum. There were over 40 different types of New Age classes. Instead of paying tuition most of the students could trade a skill or service for their classes.

TWENTY-TWO

UNUSUAL PERSPECTIVES

To perceive life through inner realization of life can be unusual. To see the astral plane can be exciting and enlightening. The astral plane has beautiful, pastel colors and spectacular, astral images. Awakened souls can see the astral plane.

We develop new perspectives and become aware of inter-dimensions which are magnificent as well as spectacular. Our experiences in awakening to God's creations and life forces are motion, light, magnetism, cohesion, inherent energy and polarities of positive and negative. Cohesion holds life together with balanced perspectives.

A distant view of a vision can be unusual. The art of picturing objects or a scene in a special way creates unusual perspectives. A specific point of view in understanding or judging things in a true relationship is an awareness of ideas and attitudes in their true perspective.

Unusual perspectives occur to alert individuals who have acquired extrasensory perception. Such an individual can see beyond a distant hill or beyond a brilliant sunset. Unusual perspectives have been seen from aerial views and even outer space. Telescopes are used to view unusual scenes in space.

Imagine walking up a volcanic mountain to watch how lava flows and spreads during an eruption. You would probably see how hot lava moves to distant locations. Lava travels into the ocean and eventually cools off. The lava becomes volcanic soil. Lava forms into land. From high mountains a person can see unusual views from quite a distance.

Horizons at the edge of oceans are spectacular. Gleaming light shines across the horizon certain times of the day. Artists create unusual perspectives in oil and water color scenes of the ocean and various landscapes of valleys, deserts and mountains, etc. Foregrounds and distant views in paintings and photographs may look unusual.

TWENTY THREE
THE LIGHTHOUSE

Maggie Jordan walked down to a lighthouse in a harbor near where she lived in Springville. This lighthouse was quite tall with a lookout tower at the top. The conical wall was thick. Maggie walked up a winding staircase with at least 175 steps to the top of the tower to look out at the magnificent view of the ocean in the harbor. She could see for miles to the horizon at the edge of the deep blue ocean in the harbor. She could also see many miles across the landscape along the coast.

Waves splashed on the rocky platform on which the lighthouse regally stood. Large beacon lights illuminated the top cabin where the lighthouse keeper lived and kept a lookout for ships in distress especially on stormy days. At night time, the powerful beacon lights flashed across the harbor to warn ships to be on the lookout for rocks, hazards, shallows and also for land which was close by. Maggie liked to sit on the beach at night to look at the lighthouse and observe the lighthouse keeper, the lights of the beacon flashing across the harbor. On foggy nights the beacon lights flashed more frequently to warn the captains and navigators of the ships, who might be struggling to see the rocks and landings through the thick fog. The lighthouse keeper even sounds the horn to warn passersby that land was nearby. Maggie watched the beacon lights flashing for several hours. She saw a tour boat arrive in the harbor. The passengers were watching a show and Katherine Grayson sang the Harbor Lights song. "I saw the harbor lights; they never told us we were parting. Maggie also gazed at the Moon and observed the deep craters. She saw the Moon and stars in the clear, night sky.

The lighthouse continued to be useful for many years. Then one night because she didn't see the beacon lights flashing any the beacon lights were not on. The captains and crewmen were unable to see the coastline from the harbor. The beacon light in the lighthouse had burned out. So, the flashing, beacon light was unable to function. Maggie and many of the other passengers were concerned when they noticed that the beacon lights were not on. The lighthouse had been a wonderful source of light and service for so many years. No one thought it would ever stop being useful.

Maggie stopped going on her night walk to see the lighthouse because she didn't see the beacon lights flashing any more. She missed the lights that used to flash frequently, lighting up the harbor and shoreline. Time passed by. One day several weeks later, Maggie decided to walk over to look at the lighthouse. She walked up the spiral staircase to the upper tower. She knocked on the cabin door and entered. She gazed out of the lighthouse window to take in the spectacular view. She enjoyed being in the lighthouse again. The beacon lights were still not flashing across the harbor. Maggie continued to look around at the view across the harbor. She wished the beacon lights would come on again. After she stood there for about an hour, something suddenly happened. The beacon lights came on and began to flash brightly across the harbor.

Maggie was overjoyed and excited when she observed the beacon lights were flashing in the harbor. She was there for nearly an hour before the lights came on fully to flash brightly. Maggie was about to leave when a young man, who was tall with dark hair and brown eyes suddenly appeared in the top tower cabin. He appeared to be friendly. He walked over to Maggie and asked, "What are you doing here?" Maggie replied, "I like this lighthouse. The beacon lights are back on." The young man said, "I know about the beacon lights, because I replaced the lights after rewiring the electric wires carefully."

Maggie stared at him. She then asked, "Do you work in this lighthouse regularly?" He replied, "I am the lighthouse attendant. I have just started working here." Maggie thought about what he had said. She said, "The beacon lights have not been turned on for weeks. I am glad that you fixed the beacon lights." He smiled and said, "I'm glad

I was able to do the electrical repairs. The beacon lights will be turned on and functioning every night from now on." Maggie responded, "Good. I missed the beacon lights coming from the lighthouse. Many other people have missed the beacon lights, too, especially the ships' captains and crewmen."

Maggie started to leave the lighthouse. The young man stopped her. He asked, "Will you be coming back to this lighthouse soon?" Maggie smiled at him and replied, "Yes, I may be back tomorrow." He smiled at Maggie and said, "Good. I hope to see you tomorrow. I will be here."

Maggie started down the stairs. She left the lighthouse in order to go home. She thought about him. She was attracted to him. She was 24 years old. She had auburn hair and hazel-brown eyes. She had a beautiful figure. Maggie walked along the beach. Then she went home after observing the Moon and stars.

The next day was Sunday. Maggie went to church in the morning. Then she did some shopping. She took her groceries home. Then Maggie had a mid afternoon snack. She decided to go for a walk on the beach. Then she walked over to the lighthouse. She entered the downstairs. The young man was doing some paper work at a desk. Maggie walked over to him and said, "Hi. I have come back." He responded, "Hi. I'm glad you're here. I have a lonely job. I am here by myself all the time." Maggie looked at him warmly. She said, "I would like to get to know you better."

The young man said, "Fine. My name is Eric Brigman. I live in Springville. I went to the elementary and high school here. I am attending college to earn a teaching degree and certificate. I'm in my last year of college." Maggie listened intently to Eric. She replied, "I grew up in Springville, too. I also went to elementary and high school in Springville. I have attended college. I have my degree in Library Science. What type of teacher are you planning to become?" Eric replied, "I plan to teach high school History."

Maggie said, "I graduated in June of this year. I am working at the public library in Springville." Eric responded, "I hope to get a job teaching History at Springville High School." Maggie responded, "You won't have to work here at the lighthouse for ever once you become a History teacher." Eric looked at Maggie warmly. He said, "You are right. I am looking forward to becoming a History teacher. I like to be around people." Maggie and Eric continued to become acquainted.

Eric showed Maggie different places in the lighthouse. They also went up to the cabin up to the top of the tower. Eric turned on the beacon light. The light flashed across the sky on to the harbor. Then Eric spoke to Maggie. "I will have two days off starting tomorrow. Would you go to lunch with me?" Maggie answered "Yes, I'll have lunch with you." Eric said, "I will pick you up at 11.45 a.m. Where shall I pick you up?" Maggie gave Eric her address and explained to him how to get to her home. She gave him her phone number as well. She looked forward to dating Eric.

Eric dated Maggie regularly for many months. They fell in love. Eventually Eric proposed marriage to Maggie. They were married and had a happy life together. They recalled that they had met at the lighthouse.

TWENTY-FOUR

LEMURS SURVIVE IN MADAGASCAR

According to Allison Jolly, Lemurs have black, bat-like ears and over-size teeth. It chisels nuts with its leaves—like incisors. Lemurs have black and silver hair and gargoyle faces. They live in blue-green, rain forests which step down to the turquoise sea.

Lemurs have very large heads in comparison to other animals. A lemur has a black, ostrich-plume tail. Diamond-shaped markings are enclosed in amber eyes outlined in black. Shimmering silver-tipped guard hairs merged with black fur and blended on head and shoulders into a base layer of pale cream.

With Lemurs sensitive ears, it can hear insect larvae move within decaying trees. It gnaws into a concealed grub and pulps with its skinny claw. The lemur is also Madagascar's equivalent of the raccoon. Lemurs raid sweet crops like coconuts and sugarcane.

Lemurs make a loud bellowing sound and a roaring alarm call. Their alerting sounds can be heard throughout the forest. They use their black, bell-rope tails to perch on tree tops. Most lemurs have a single offspring at a time. Some lemurs bear litters of one to five young, which grow within months to independence.

Twenty-five years ago French naturalist and the dozens of lemur watchers, Jean-Jacques letter, of the National Museum of Natural

History in Paris, estimated that only 50 lemurs might survive. He feared their fate as a species was sealed.

Lemurs are primates, like monkeys, apes and us. Humans share with lemurs a mutual squirrel size mammal that surveyed the subtropical forests at least 50 million years ago with forward-facing eyes supported by a pillar of facial bone. They projected from its hands and nails tipped its fingers, just as in lemurs of today, its living descendants.

Ancestors of lemurs first appeared more than 40 million years ago, rafting on branches or logs across the strait to Madagascar which had begun itself from Africa 125 million years earlier. Without primate competition the lemur now composes 28 species and 40 races found nowhere else.

Mouse lemurs, reclusive and nocturnal, feed on fruits and insects. Red-bellied lemurs form monogamous pairs until humans arrived about 1,500 years ago Madagascar supported more than a dozen species of giant lemurs, which shortly became extinct. They face tremendous odds. The people of Madagascar are impoverished. They slash, burn and saw these trees in order to create croplands. They have reduced Madagascar's rain forest by half since 1950 leaving lemurs with less forests to live in.

The village president of Ivontaka said, "You know in a town south of here the river has dried up for the first time in living memory, because of deforestation." The Malagasy are learning that conservation can avoid destroying their own environment. To assure the future of lemurs, much more needs to be learned about their behavior. We need to know the physical space lemurs require. Behavioral knowledge of lemurs offers insights into the earliest origins of a group life among our ancestors.

Intense study of lemur society began in 1963. Primate studies reported that males dominated females. However, every female in her troop took precedence over males when feeding. Among the monogamous indri, the female browses succulent, treetop leaves while her mate waits in the forked, lower branches. If his patience wears thin and he climbs higher, she cuffs him back to his place.

Lemur's code of female rights may stem from their brief mating seasonal. Males fight to compete for mating season. One male may mate with three females or more usually in April after mating males are exhausted. Males are gashed on their flank thigh or ear by other males.

If a female does not conceive, she may come into heat again in a month or two. Breeding cycles leave lemur mothers pregnant or lactating in the harshest seasons.

In southern Madagascar, July is dry and cold. Young lemurs and poor Malagasy children alike wheeze with bronchitis and die of pneumonia. September is dusty and hot. In deciduous forests, trees stand leafless. At dawn pregnant ringtails lick dew from bare branches. At noon they drape themselves panting in the trees. At dusk they slip to a stream to gulp water, alert for hawks hunting along the banks. Not until cool darkness descends do the mothers give birth. Ringtail females need every scrap of food they or their mates can find.

A few trees develop flowers and fruit in time to produce seeds for November rains. A ringtail troop is clearly a matriarchy. Daughters remain with the mothers who bear them and the aunts who help raise them. If another troop approaches, Amazons fly at the intruders, babies on their backs, to defend their territory and larder. All but two female white sifakas tagged in 1984 have so far stayed in their original groups. However, many males have jumped troops one or more times each year.

Lemurs have no trouble identifying members of their own troop or even those of other groups. Lemurs, like monkeys, have social knowledge and social uses of intelligence. However, they lack the cleverness of monkeys in handling objects.

Once lemurs were the size of great apes. The mouse lemur weighs less than three ounces. This species lives in eastern rain forests and loves to eat berries. Since humans first reached Madagascar, 14 species of lemurs have disappeared, nearly all larger than those who live today. Their skeletal remains tell us that one rivaled a gorilla in size and was probably earthbound by its great weight. Two species ran on the ground, one slender and fleet, the other stockier and slower.

Bamboo lemurs are mammals best known, being the giant panda that can digest fibrous, giant grass. Small, gray bamboo lemurs have been sighted off and on for decades. However, their cousin has vanished about a century ago. Three bamboo-eating species are now known. All range in the eastern rainforest, where the proposed Ranomafana National Park may preserve 100,000 acres of habitats.

TWENTY-FIVE

AUTHENTIC INSIGHTS

Authentic insights occur when a soul realizes higher consciousness. As the consciousness of a soul expands extraordinary thoughts may take place. For instance, Buddhism awareness awakens the soul presence and Christ consciousness awakens the soul presence to God reality and God illumination.

Expanded awareness inspires a soul to think much deeper awareness. Day by day, year by year a soul can attain spiritual growth through meditation. Authentic insights may develop to illumine a soul to become One with God and all good.

Guatama Buddha, Jesus Christ, Yogananda, Krishna and Mahatma Ghandi were spiritual adepts who experienced authentic insights. They also lived spiritual lives of spiritual illumination and service. When authentic insights emerge the higher mind vibrates and communicates at a much higher level because the soul listens to the still, small voice within. Authentic insights help souls mature spiritually. Every thought, word and deed performed with sincere action helps a soul progress spiritually on a spiritual path. Authentic insights help souls mature spiritually. Every thought, word and deed performed with sincere action helps a soul progress spiritually on a spiritual path.

TWENTY-SIX

THE NARROW ESCAPE

One day I drove to a beautiful lagoon in Oceano, California. I parked my car perpendicular to the lagoon which was 40 feet to 50 feet deep. I had parked near the lagoon many times in the past. On a previous occasion I got into an accident here when I swerved off the road at the bridge I was crossing. This day I viewed the lagoon for approximately forty-five minutes.

I turned on my car motor to leave. I put my car gear in reverse to back up. My gear shift jammed. My car went forward instead of backwards. My car was moving towards the deep level of the lagoon. My car brakes didn't work properly. I was unable to stop my car. I decided to veer my car wheels left to go in a different direction. I continued to put my foot on the brake. My brakes didn't work. I didn't think fast enough to pull the hand brake.

My car went down a ravine into the lagoon. Fortunately, I was able to turn my wheels left into thick reeds. My car stopped in the reeds which had thick bamboo roots. Part of my car submerged in the edge of the lagoon. Within minutes lagoon water came up above the floorboard into the car. I tried to open the front door. The door jammed into the reeds. I was unable to get out of the car. My purse and script writings fell to the floor from the front passenger seat. My script was flooded with water. I grabbed my purse within minutes and put it on the passenger seat.

I was in a state of shock because my car could have gone into the deep end of the lagoon. I had a very narrow escape from drowning in the deep end of the lagoon. I screamed for help. It took around five minutes before a young couple came over to help me.

The man tried to get me out of the car. Finally, he called 911. It took fifteen minutes for an ambulance with paramedics to arrive. Eventually, policemen arrived. Meanwhile, the lady took my purse and script and placed them on the lawn. Several paramedics walked over to my car. They tried to get me out of the car. They used a canvas chair for me to sit on after they pulled me out of my car.

My legs and feet were stuck in the lagoon and reeds. I had difficulty climbing up the ravine after I stepped out of the lagoon to the canvas chair. The paramedics expected me to walk up the ravine once they lifted me in the canvas chair to the edge of the ravine. I managed to walk up the ravine with assistance. I walked over to a tree log to sit down

An officer from the California Highway Patrol walked up to me. He asked for my driver's license. I took out my driver's license and handed it to the officer. He sat in his police car for about twenty minutes writing up what he thought happened. He didn't ask me any questions before he wrote his report.

I waited while I continued to sit on a log. I asked if anyone could take me home. No one offered to give me a ride home. Four police cars were parked nearby. An ambulance and fire engine and people were on the lawn near the lagoon. Yet, no one offered to take me home.

Another policeman questioned me while I was still stuck in my car. This policeman wasn't helping me get out of my car when he saw water rising in it. I told him I needed help out of my car before I would answer any questions. He acted like a robot without feeling what I was going through. I needed to be rescued from a dangerous situation before explaining what had happened to cause the accident.

The CHP officer finally came back and handed me a pink paper. He didn't return my license. Naturally, I was upset and I felt he was treating me badly and unfairly. I told him that I thought he was being very unfair.

Some friends happened to be driving in the area. They saw the ambulance truck, fire engine and police cars parked near the lagoon. They saw people standing around. Then, they saw me sitting on a log.

I called my friends. They walked over to me and asked what happened. I told them about how my car malfunctioned. I told them I needed a ride home. They said they would take me home. I was so grateful that these friends had arrived unexpectedly.

I walked over to their car and sat in the front passenger seat. Fortunately, I was not injured from the accident. The reeds in the lagoon cushioned my car. It was a few seconds for me to think of turning into the reeds, which saved my life. I am grateful for the narrow escape. If my car had gone into the deep part of the lagoon it would have caused the car to sink into the lagoon. I may not have been able to get my car door open in time to avoid drowning in the car.

I read the false report the CHP officer wrote about the accident. He made up an excuse that he was supposed to write me up and take away my license. After reading the false report, I called the CHP Office and complained about the false report. I wrote a response to explain what really happened during the accident. I gave my written report to a safety inspector at DMV (Department of Motor Vehicles). He read my report; plus he tape recorded my verbal statement about my car accident.

The CHP officer had filled out a reevaluation paper which meant I had to take the DMV drivers test, vision test, DMV regular-drivers test and submit a DMV medical report. I passed all these tests. My driver's license was mailed back to me from the CHP Office.

What an ordeal to go through especially when the accident was caused because my car malfunctioned! I was grateful to be alive, plus not be injured from this accident. I definitely had a narrow escape from death

It took three weeks for my car to be repaired. I had to ask friends to drive me around so I could go to appointments, go shopping and go to social activities as well as to church. In the countryside, bus service is too far away. A person must walk for miles to a bus stop. Then people wait at least an hour for a bus to arrive.

Drivers should have their cars checked closely every three months to have their gear shift, brakes, tie rods, transmission, tires and other car parts checked and repaired. You should be sure your car is safe to drive.

TWENTY-SEVEN
USE YOUR IMAGINATION

Everyone has an opportunity to develop his or her imagination. A person's mind continues to create thoughts. Visual images go through the third eye frequently. The human mind is capable of being creative.

Thoughts create images. Images are interesting to visualize. Images continue to change. Color schemes can be colorful and fascinating to observe.

Writers, artists, architects, gourmet cooks and clothes designers use their imagination. Writers can use ideas in stories, plays, novels and articles to visualize imaginary experiences, places and relationships with characters. Artists recreate artistic expressions of nature. They observe vivid colors, contrast of colors and shapes. Artists develop perspective in landscapes and geometries.

Gourmet cooks are creative in the way they accumulate ingredients and combine different recipes. Herbs, oils, salt, pepper and sauces are added to ingredients. Vegetables and fruits are chopped up and shredded and combined. Then herbs, oils and various sauces are added. Many delicious recipes have been created. Gourmet cooks are able to create many new recipes. They use their imagination.

Clothes designers use their imagination to design clothes. They are capable of creating designs of a variety of dresses, pant suits, slacks, coats, sweaters, jackets and swimming suits. Some seamstresses create lingerie such as underpants, slips and bras. Night gowns, pajamas and bathrobes are also designed with creative designs.

There are many ways to use our imagination. People, who are creative in the world, use their imagination. So, make an effort to use your imagination. You are capable of developing creative projects and experiencing creative interests and hobbies if you pursue creative goals.

TWENTY-EIGHT

THE DOLL HOUSE

Sara Sheldon was five years old. She liked to play with dolls. Her parents gave her a variety of dolls to play with. She kept her dolls in her bedroom. Sara spent a lot of time playing with her dolls. She combed their hair and dressed them. She talked to her dolls and treated them like playmates.

Sara kept her dolls on her play table and her bed. She wished she had a big doll house to put her dolls in. She had twenty dolls. Sara told her Mother she wanted a doll house. Her mother told her that someone would have to build a dollhouse. Her father was not a carpenter. Perhaps, someone they knew would build a doll house.

Sara's mother asked different friends and relatives if they could build a dollhouse. Finally, a friendly neighborhood heard that Sara wanted a dollhouse. He offered to build a large dollhouse built. He gathered wood, nails and carpenter tools. Then, he made a building plan.

The neighbors name was Sam Goodman. He appeared to know how to build a doll house. Sam developed a floor plan. Then he developed a framework to the dollhouse. Next, he built a wooden roof. Each room in the dollhouse was built. He nailed wood sidings to the walls inside and outside of the dollhouse. Once the floors and walls were completed Sam painted the walls first. Then he used a wood stain on the wood floors.

There were six rooms in the new dollhouse. The outside of the dollhouse was painted gold. The roof was a green and red color. The dollhouse was large enough to store all of Sara's dolls. She had wood, plastic and rubber dolls. They all had beautiful sewn in hair. Each doll had pink cheeks. Several dolls had dark skin.

Sara selected attractive clothes for her dolls to wear. She changed their clothes often. Sara placed her dolls in the new dollhouse in different rooms. She was happy to have a dollhouse to keep her dolls in. Sara thanked Sam Goodman for building a large dollhouse for her. The dollhouse was placed in a large playroom in her parents' home. Sara was able to step into the large dollhouse to play with her dolls. She played with her dolls frequently. She changed diapers on dolls which wet their diapers. She pretended to feed them. She put them to bed.

Sara was grateful that her parents asked someone to build a dollhouse for her dolls. Sara invited her friends to play in her new dollhouse with her and her dolls.

TWENTY-NINE

SEA FARERS

Seafarers go to sea regularly to travel to distant places. They learn to work on ships and vessels as crewmen. The crew helps to tie ropes, pull up sails, clean ship decks and to keep the ships clean and neat.

Seafarers must adjust to storms at sea. The ship will sway side ways and up and down. Waves splash onto the ship decks. The ship may be covered with ocean currents. Crewmen must hold on to planks and stay inside ship cabins. They need to remain as calm as possible during ocean storms. Waves tend to rise very high in the ocean. Crewmen must work quickly to scoop water off the decks.

The Captain needs to keep the ship from capsizing. He must steer the ship carefully passed the high, rough waves. Crewmen work down below in the coal room on ships run with coal and wood in large stove burners to keep the burners producing light and heat as well as fuel to keep ships moving at sea.

Seafarers learn to survive for along time at sea. The climate may change suddenly. He may be hot with piercing sunlight. Then clouds form and rain comes pouring down. Waves move up and down and ripple in the ocean. Wind blows swiftly and may produce cold weather in a period of hours.

Seafarers learn to use compasses and binoculars while they are at sea. They also use spyglasses to see far away. There are spectacular views at sea. The horizon is interesting to observe. There may be a colorful sunset near the horizon above the ocean. Bright sunlight may beam along the horizon.

Seafarers travel frequently across oceans and seas to different landscapes. Seafarers are explorers and adventurers. They want to cross the ocean to new places. They are curious about going to different places. Seafarers spend a lot of time at sea. Some seafarers learn about fauna and sea plants. Some seafarers fish at sea. They catch many types of fish. Some fish are very large and some are much smaller. Seafarers may also catch whales, sea otters and seals at sea. They wear fur coats, jackets and pants. They also wear leather boots up to their knees as well as rubber boots. Rubber boots are handy especially on wet boats and ships.

Seafarers will always exist as long as oceans and seas exist. They will continue to go across the oceans and seas to explore and navigate on the oceans and seas. Since ancient time's seafarers have traveled in boats, canoes, Viking boats and Egyptian boats, etc.

THIRTY

SIBERIA, A VAST
LAND IN RUSSIA

Siberia is located in Russia in the upper, northern area. Siberia is fifty times larger than the United States of America. The landscape varies in Siberia.

There are villages and cities in Siberia. However, there are vast landscapes which are uninhabitable. There is a lot of volcanic landscape. Poisonous gases deplete the oxygen. Trees die because of poisonous gases that seep out of the ground in upper Siberia.

Purple bacteria turn the water pink. The water smells like rotten eggs. The water becomes stagnate. Then the fish die out because they need oxygen. Lava layers were thousands of layers deep. Methane gas is spread into the atmosphere. It is believed that the lava inside the Earth in Siberia will one day spread in such a way to cause tsunamis in the oceans which will cause flooding and severe destruction.

Yet, there are beautiful locations in Siberia. There are some forests, wild flowers, rivers and some waterfalls. From late April to September it does not snow. Spring occurs during late April and throughout the summer.

Much of Siberia is in tundra country where trees do not grow. Wild flowers grow in meadows and fields. The temperature goes down to minus 30 degrees below zero and even much lower.

Tomsk is one of the most enjoyable cities in Siberia. At least 500,000 people live there. There are fine wooden mansions, old commercial buildings and a dynamic modern outlook. There are beautiful flowers and marvelous waterways.

Tomsk is a university city and has a half dozen major academic establishments. Tomsk was closed during the Soviet period. It is open to foreigners today. The downtown area is called Lenina and is an architectural and entertainment smorgasbord dotted with restaurants, bars and shops. Some wooden architecture is the Hunter House, Russian-German House, Dragon House, Peacock House, Kirous House, Shishor-House, Znameniye, Bozhyey Maataeri Church and Sshkoola School.

Other sites are a fortress on Ressurrection Hill,Tomsk History Museums, a lookout tower, Voznessenskaya Church, Ogero Beloye Pond and Old Believers' Wood Church. Central Leninha is a collection of beautifully restored historic buildings.

Cafes and great architecture continue in areas such as Nakhanovicha where there is the Tomsk Art Gallery. The Atashev Palace was built for gold-mining entrepreneur, Ivan Atasher in 1842. Low rooms host the Regional Museum with a few Atashev furnishings.

There are spectacular views along the Tom River. Religious buildings Trinity church, Nevsky Church, Peter and Paul Cathedral, the White Mosque and Red Mosque.

Barnal, the capital of the Altai Territory, is a prosperous, industrial city. It has the nearest, major airport in the Altai Republic. Barnaul offers enough cafes and museums to amuse visitors.

Artybash is in Siberia. It consists of a pretty ribbon of cottages, home stays and mini hotels along the Teetskoya to the currently closed Turbaza Zaltoe Ozera. At Lake Teletskooes westernmost nose, little Logach village is the main population center and bus stop. Karbu-Waterfalls are fairly memorable experiences. Speedboats go on Lake Taletskoe. This lake freezes during winter. The village becomes a winter wonderland.

There are other villages such as Mazherek, Chemal, Chysky Trakt, Kemerovo. Rach village is unique with interesting architecture. The Siberian villagers have traditional folkways, artistic paintings, carved woodwork and folk dances. Siberia is a fascinating province in Russia.

THIRTY-ONE

POLITICAL ISSUES THAT CONCERN AMERICAN CITIZENS

American citizens are concerned about political issues such as depletion of the American economy, wars in the Middle East and lack of enough employment in America. Americans are concerned that billions of dollars are spent on wars in Iraq, Afghanistan and other Middle Eastern countries. Why should American monies be depleted in this manner?

Inflation of the American dollar has been another concern of the American people. The value of the American dollar is approximately 50 percent. If the American dollar was valued at 95 percent its value would help Americans to buy more goods and services. Their wages and savings would have much more value. Americans could spend more money. They would save more money for emergencies.

The wars in the Middle East have gone on for nearly nine years. A great deal of money has been spent by America to pay for warfare weapons, for wages to the Armed Services and for many supplies. Billions of dollars are used for wars and cause American schools to have far less funds to pay for supplies, teacher salaries, school maintenance, etc. One Hundred Seventy teachers have been given pink slips this May, 2010, in San Luis Obispo County. They were laid off because there isn't enough money in the California State budget to pay them salaries. This should not be happening. Education is very important.

Classroom sizes have increased considerably because there are less teachers to teach students. The usual classroom size is 28 to 30 students. Now classroom sizes are 38 to 40 students in each classroom. The larger the classroom load is, means teachers can't give as much time to each student on a one to one basis.

The quality of education is vital so that Americans, who are well educated, can help improve our way of life in America. Enough money is needed to secure the improvement of American education.

Americans are concerned about keeping their jobs. At least 25 to 30 percent of the population are unemployed. Americans need to remain employed and to receive opportunities to work. They need to be employed to receive monthly and annual wages. More and more businesses are folding up because of the cost of expenses to keep their businesses open. This means that less and less are employed. The billions of dollars spent on the wars depletes the American budget and energy money.

Jobs should be created with government, financial help. More money should be available in the American Treasury to provide employment for Americans.

Another concern is that many immigrants have been coming into America. They take up jobs that Americans need. Some are illegal immigrants who are sneaking into America. They are willing to work for less than the minimum wage. So, they are employed in place of Americans. This should not be happening in America. Americans should have opportunities to receive employment.

Big bankers have been given millions of dollars from the American government. They have kept large sums for themselves. The monies banks have been given comes from American taxes and the American Treasury. Millions of dollars could be used to create more employment and to feed impoverished, starving children and adults in America. Money can be used for better housing for homeless people.

Big bankers who keep large sums of American government money should be punished for taking money dishonestly. They should have to return all the money they have taken.

THIRTY-TWO

THE PATIO ARRANGEMENT

Shelley Lehman liked to spend time outdoors. She worked in her garden. She had a large front and back yard. However, there was no cement or rock patio. Shelley wanted a patio to be created in the backyard. She measured her backyard. She wanted a large, cement mixture with rocks spread over the leveled, smoothed out ground.

Once a cement foundation was spread out in the backyard, Shelley had the foundation painted beige. She placed colorful, large, garden pots around the patio foundation. Colorful flowers were arranged in each pot. The color of each pot blended with the patio arrangements. Shelley decided to add garden tables and chairs in the patio.

After the patio had been arranged carefully, Shelley decided to sit in a garden chair. She gazed at her garden of roses, daisies, camellias, lilacs, nasturtiums, petunias, hyenas and more. She enjoyed the fragrance of the flowers and fresh air. She felt a cool breeze blow a rose in her face. The sunshine gleamed on the flowers, grass and tree leaves. Shelley felt relaxed and at peace while she sat in her backyard patio. Shelley decided to invite her friends over to sit in her patio. Harry, Virginia and Rose came over to enjoy Shelley's garden. Shelley served mint, herb tea and cookies to them as they sat in patio chairs around a table in the patio. They observed flowers bobbing in the breeze. Bees and butterflies were flying around. They landed on different flowers. Hummingbirds fluttered their wings as they came into the garden.

Whippoorwills, robins and meadowlarks were chirping nearby. Blue Jays flew into the garden. Shelley had placed a bird feeder on a pole in her garden. Birds flew over to the bird feeder to pluck bird seeds.

Shelley had a pleasant time with her friends in her new patio. She invited friends to come over to enjoy her new patio. Her friends were impressed with Shelley's patio arrangement. Shelley continued to enjoy her backyard patio especially on warm, sunny days. She felt refreshed and restored after she sat in her patio. She was glad she had arranged her patio with colorful, potted flowers. The patio tables and chairs were very useful. Shelley felt renewed when she was outdoors. The fragrance of her garden, fresh air and sunshine had a healing effect.

THIRTY-THREE

SANTA CLAUS IS COMING TO TOWN

Santa Claus is coming to town! Santa Claus is coming to town! Santa Claus comes at Christmas time with gifts for many children and even adults. Saint Nicolas existed in Europe. Saint Nicolas gave gifts to needy families at Christmas time.

Many young children believe that Santa Claus exists when they are 2, 3, 4, 5 and even 6 years old. They believe he lands on their roof at their home. If there is a chimney, Santa Claus climbs down into the living room with a bag of gifts. Santa Claus places gifts on the mantle and under the Christmas tree.

Then Santa Claus climbs up the chimney and gets back into his sleigh. His reindeer fly up in the sky off the roof to deliver gifts to other children. Santa Claus has made a list of gifts children wish for which he continues to deliver.

Santa Claus tells children they must be good and well behaved in order to receive gifts at Christmas time. Christmas has been celebrated for over one thousand years. Christmas began in Europe in England, Germany, The Netherlands, Switzerland, Austria and France, etc. There are Christmas parades, Christmas parties, Christmas plays and downtown Christmas celebrations. Santa Claus attends these celebrations. Christmas carols are sung and delicious goodies are served during Christmas time. Every year everyone looks forward to Santa Claus to come to town.

THIRTY-FOUR
MOSAIC DESIGNS

Mosaic stone designs are unique. Mosaic designs are laid out on bathroom, shower floors and walls. Each mosaic design is different. A variety of colors are used. Different shapes are also used. The combinations of colors, shapes and sizes affect the mosaic patterns.

Triangles, rectangles and squares are used with mosaic stones to place together closely to create new designs such as flowers, ocean scenes, people, landscapes and geometric designs. Bright colors can be combined to add to exotic and interesting patterns.

Mosaics can be made with colored paper designs which are pasted to a cardboard platform or thick chartboard. Mosaic designs look good on kitchen walls, bedroom walls, lounge room walls and in public buildings.

Mosaic designs have been used for thousands of years. Mosaic designs were used by the Romans, Sumerians, Egyptians, Israelites, Babylonians and other Persian locations. Persian temples are completely designed with mosaic, interior designs. Blue, turquoise and white mosaic stones are placed closely together. Thousands of mosaic stones are made and used. They are glued down tightly.

Churches in Europe also use mosaic stones on church walls. Many walls look colorful and unique with mosaic designs. Mosaics are still popular today. Many tile stores sell mosaic stones and mosaic designs.

THIRTY-FIVE

UNUSUAL OCCASIONS

Unusual occasions may occur when we least expect them to take place. A celebration may occur because of a celebrity war hero. A writers' group may have a book review day in the park. A nutrition and health day may be sponsored in the park. A Scouts' Day may take place unexpectedly.

All in all, unusual occasions surprise and motivate us. The birth of a new born baby excites people who know the parents. A sudden boat race may take place. A large picnic may take place on the beach or the park.

Unusual occasions excite and surprise us. Such occasions help us experience extraordinary happenings so we can overcome an ordinary, dull life. Sudden, unexpected experiences make life interesting.

THIRTY-SIX

LASTING MEMORIES

Lasting memories are very special experiences which have made an impact on us. We remember important occasions and special experiences. Some lasting memories are very happy experiences. Other lasting memories may be unhappy memories.

Lasting memories affect our feelings and realization of life on a regular basis. We recall how our memorable experiences, dreams and ideas change our lives. Without significant memories to recall, our lives would not be meaningful. Our memories are stored in our memory bank or subconscious. We learn from our memories.

We need to recall what we have learned in our daily lives in order to relate to others and to survive. For instance, we learn to talk, to read and write and to develop specific academic skills in order to live in the world using our intelligence.

Everything we learn about our world, community life and family life help us learn to help relate and survive on Earth. We must learn to recall our memories about what we have learned in our parents' home, at school and in our community. If we forget many things we need to remember in order to be independent. We become dependent on others to help us.

Amnesia causes a person to forget his past. People with amnesia usually forget people, places, basic learning skills and past events. Until they overcome amnesia they don't respond to the past. They must start over again and remember what they once knew. This takes reliving which may take time to recall and to remember.

So, treasure your memories and strengthen your memory bank so that you can recall important memories. You will relate better in the world if you recall lasting memories that are meaningful.

THIRTY-SEVEN

MIRAGES

Mirages appear in the distance and they seem real. As a person approaches the location where the mirage was it has disappeared. The image or mirage was a figment of the person's imagination.

People who travel in the desert quite often see images or mirages of an oasis with palm trees, or a large palace gleaming in the sunlight, or other caravans moving towards the travelers. Mirages elude a person's mind because he or she may imagine something they want to see.

Wishful thinking causes travelers to see mirages. When they approach the place where the mirage once existed they are surprised and disappointed that the mirage has disappeared.

Mirages may be very interesting or very disturbing. They are usually in the distance. Some mirages may be up close. The closer a mirage appears, the more real it seems to be. Could a parallel image exist where the mirage occurred? Could the mirage be appearing from another plane temporarily to alert travelers from other dimensions?

THIRTY-EIGHT

FAMILY ALBUMS

Family albums are developed and kept with many family photos. Each family photographed may be labeled. It helps to keep labeled photographs so that dates such as months and year and name of people and places are written on the outside of each photograph.

Great grandparents, aunts, uncles, parents, brothers and sisters, cousins and nephews and nieces, as well as friends and acquaintances are placed in the family album. Photographs bring back fond memories of years gone by.

Photographs help us remember special moments in our lives. When we can go through a family album, the history of our family can be revealed. So, from time to time it is worthwhile to look through your family album to enjoy viewing family photographs.

THIRTY-NINE
THE HIDDEN TREASURES

Hidden treasures exist under the oceans in sunken ships. These treasures were on pirate ships, Spanish galleons and English and French ships. Many of these ships have disappeared under the ocean.

Millions of dollars of treasures such as gold rings, necklaces, bracelets and anklets, diamond rings, necklaces and bracelets and silver and gold goblets, trays, plates, cups and saucers are under the ocean.

Hidden treasures are being rediscovered because different people are going under the ocean to find lost ships. They are able to find treasures in these deserted ships. Different people are able to clean up treasures once they bring them up from the ocean.

Other treasures hidden in the ocean are sapphires, rubies, opals and emeralds. When these precious gems are polished they sparkle and gleam. These precious gems are cut and put in rings, brocades and necklaces. These treasures are very valuable.

The hidden treasures are sold to buyers who wear jewelry selected from the treasures. The jewelry looks elegant and colorful. A diamond necklace may cost thousands of dollars. A diamond ring and gold ring can be very expensive. Even jade, emeralds, rubies, opals and sapphires can be quite expensive once they are cut, polished and formed into jewelry.

Gold and silver can be found in caves. Gold may be hidden inside thick, cave walls. Miners dig deep in cave walls to find gold. Silver is discovered in silver mines. Diamonds are found in diamond mines in deep caves. Gold, silver and diamonds are hidden before they are found.

FORTY

THE KOLBRIN BIBLE

The KOLBRIN BIBLE is an ancient, secular, academic work. It offers alternate accounts of several stories from the HOLY BIBLE and other wisdom texts. The Kolbrin Bible accurately defines the work and also has it in a civilization that played a critical role in its dissemination.

The term "Bible" comes from the Greek "Bilia" meaning books, which stems from the Greek "Byblos." Byblos was an ancient, Phoenecian port located in what is now the central coast of Lebanon. The Phoenicians imported papyrus from Egypt and sold it abroad along with ancient wisdom texts. The KOLBRIN BIBLE was called THE GREAT BOOK.

THE GREAT BOOK was originally written in Hieratic by Egyptian academics, after the Exodus of the Jews (1500 BCE). Its original 21 volumes were later translated using the 22 letter Phoenician alphabet, which later spawned the Greek and English alphabet of today.

The only known copy of THE GREAT BOOK to survive the millennia was the one exported to Britain by the Phoenicans in the First Century BCE. Unfortunately, much of THE GREAT BOOK was destroyed when the Glastonbury Abbey was set ablaze in 1184 BCE. The attack of the abbey was ordered by English King Henry II, after he accused the Abbey of being mystical heretics. The Celtic priests transcribed the surviving Phoenician translations to bronze sheets and stored them in copper-clad, wooden boxes. THE GREAT BOOK became known as THE BRONZE BOOK. In the 18th Century BCE the Bronze Book, was merged with a Celtic wisdom book called the COEL BOOK to become THE KOLBRIN BIBLE.

The 21st Century Master edition of THE KOLBRIN BIBLE was published for scholars. This edition is available in a letter-sized paperback with ample margins for notes. The Egyptian texts of the Bronze book is recommended for those with an interest in 2012 Mayan prophecies, Planet X (Nibiru and factual alternative accounts of Noah's Flood and Exodus and Celtic texts of the Coelbook). This Celtic text is recommended for those with an interest in Druid and Celtic philosophy and prophecies. This text also contains newly detailed, biographical accounts of Jesus Christ with several first person quotes.

The Celtics were inspired by Egyptian texts. The Celtics wrote their own historical and philosophical anthology in a similar manner, but in their own language. The Celtic texts offer a timeless insight into Druid folklore, mysticism and philosophy.

THE COEL BOOK was inspired by a visit by Jesus Christ in Britain. Jesus was possibly in his teens or middle twenties when he traveled on a Phoenician trading ship to Britain with his great Uncle Joseph of Arimethea, who undertook the journey to inspect a tin mine he owned.

Historians maintain that Jesus studied the Egyptian texts in Britain. The Celtic texts published a biography of Jesus. Historical accounts indicate Joseph of Armethea founded the Glastonbury Abbey about 36 CE and that it eventually became the repository for these texts during the first millennium.

After the attack at Glastonbury Abbey, the priests fled with what remained of these ancient works to a secret location in Scotland, where the Egyptian texts were transcribed to bronze sheets. In the 18th century the two books were combined and translated into old English to form the first identifiable edition of THE KOLBRIN BIBLE. In the 20th Century, the manuscripts were transferred to London and updated to Continental English. THE KOLBRIN BIBLE still uses the Continental English update, but has been edited according to modern rules of grammar and punctuation based on the Chicago MANUAL OF STYLE.

"To facilitate the historical study of the work, YOUR OWN

WORLD BOOKS divided the creation span into seven master editions using the criteria of publication era and country, according to Jacovan der Worp, MS Marshall Masters and Janice Manning.

THE KOLBRIN BIBLE reveals spiritual insights and wisdom so many spiritual seekers can awaken to ancient, spiritual knowledge. What remains and has been translated in different languages can enlighten and awaken many people to inner truths.

FORTY-ONE

THE MEADOWLARK

A meadowlark flew over to an elm tree and perched on a branch in a meadow. It began chirping in a high pitched voice. The meadowlark's song could be heard clearly by passers-by. Its melodic tones uplifted everyone nearby.

This meadowlark stood on the branch looking regal with its bright yellow breast, black phased collar and brown wings and feathers. The meadowlark continued to chirp cheerfully. Suddenly, a cat walked by and stared at the meadowlark. The cat listened to the meadowlark chirping. The cat was hungry. The cat wished that it could capture the meadowlark to eat because the cat was famished.

While the meadowlark continued chirping, the cat decided to climb up the trunk of the elm tree. It dug its claws into the trunk and it climbed up to a side branch. It sat on the branch quietly. The meadowlark saw the cat approaching it. The meadowlark stopped chirping. It flew away from the elm tree quickly. The meadowlark knew the cat was approaching it. The meadowlark knew cats eat birds. It flew away to avoid being attacked and eaten.

The meadowlark flew across the sky for several miles. It finally landed on the ground under some tall pine trees. The meadowlark moved around looking for seeds and berries. Then the meadowlark flew up to a pine branch. It perched on the branch.

The meadowlark began chirping beautiful melodies. Squirrels

were scurrying around in the trees and on the ground. The squirrels didn't try to attack the meadowlark. Yet, the squirrels were larger than meadowlarks.

When it became dark the meadowlark flew off to its nest to lie down to rest and sleep. There were no cats around. The meadowlark rested quietly at night. It waited until sunrise before it chirped again. Suddenly, a brown bear appeared in the pine forest. It walked through the woods. The meadowlark stopped chirping when it saw the brown bear and heard the bears' footsteps. The meadowlark flew up high into the pine trees to get away from the brown bear. The bear began climbing the pine tree. The bear shook the tree as it continued to climb higher and higher.

The meadowlark decided to fly away from the pine tree before the brown bear could capture it. It nearly fell to the ground because the bear shook the tree so swiftly. The meadowlark escaped narrowly from the brown bear. The meadowlark managed to survive. It had flown miles away from the pine forest far away from the brown bear.

The meadowlark chirped in another tree in another woodland. It saw wild rabbits, opossums and squirrels moving around in the woods. The meadowlark felt safer then than it had felt in other locations. The meadowlark continued to chirp and sing sweetly in this safer place.

FORTY-TWO

WELL KNOWN OPERAS

Opera is the Italian word for "work." Opera is a dramatic work set to music and is short for integral. In opera, the words of the play are sung by singers, who are accompanied by instruments. Singing may be interrupted by dialogue, known as recitative Italian which may be accompanied by one or more instruments.

Drama consists of solos known as arias and ensembles for two or more singers and choruses. Dramatic works have always contained some form of music. An example of incidental music written for plays is A MIDSUMMER NIGHT'S DREAM composed by MENDELSOHN. Well known operas are LA BOHEME, TANNHAUSER, GIOVANNI, CARMEN, RIGELETTO, TALE OF TWO CITIES, THE BEGGAR'S OPERA, A LIFE OF A TSAR (1836) and TEMPEST.

Opera developed with the Italian musician, Claudio Monteverdi (1567-1643). He served at the Court of the Duke of Montua as a violin player and madrigal singer. Monteverdi's first opera, LA FAVOLA d'ORFEO was produced in 1607 and was the first opera to be accompanied with a full orchestra.

In France in the same period the pioneers in opera were Jean Baptiste Lully (1632-1687) and Jean Philippe Rameau (1683-1764). After Monteverdi, the next great name in the history of opera was George Frideric Handel (1685-1759), a German who settled in England

and composed most of his operas for London between 1711 and 1741. Handel is well known for THE MESSIAH, a spiritual musical.

George Gershwin's PORGY AND BESS was an American opera which had its premier on Broadway in New York in 1935. It was the first successful, American opera. Gershwin has been followed by Virgil Thomson (1896-1989), Samuel Barber (1910 to 1981), the Italian-born Gian Carlo Menotti (1911-2007), Dominick Argento (1927) and John Adams (1947) were successful composers of opera.

Tobias Picker (1954) composed THERESE RAQUIN which was produced in Dallas in 2000 and AN AMERICAN TRAGEDY at the Metropolitan Opera House in 2005. Handel, Mozart, Strauss, Janacek, Britten, Puccini and Verdi achieved greatness in opera and other fields of music. One of opera's greats was the Czech soprano who in 1910 in New York created Minnie in Puccini's LA FANCIULLA DEL WEST. Back-stage interval, Birgit Nilsson (1918-2005) was the Dyer's Wife and Leonie Rysanek (1926-1998) was the Empress in Strauss's DIE FRAU OHNE SCHATTEN, in San Francisco in 1980. Legendary Nouve giant, Heldenopran Kirsten Glageslad was Isolla in the United States in 1937. She gave the first performance of Strauss's VIER LETZTE LIEDER in London in 1950.

The renowned English mezzo soprano Jane Baker (1933) was outstanding as Cluck's Orfeo Monteveri's Penelope and was Donizetti's Maria Sluarda. Most elegant of the lyric tenors was Alfredo Kraus (1927-1999) as Tonio in Donizetti's LA FILLE DUREGIMENT at the Metropolitan Opera in New York in 1983. Making his mark among the present generation is the Mexican Rolando Villazon (1972) seen as Massenet's Milo. Chaly poet was Werther, in Nice Opera in 2006.

During the Baroque Era in 1600 to the mid-18th century some featured operas by Monteverdi are LA FAVOLA de ORFEO (1607), RITORNO de' VISSE IN PATRIA (1640), and L'INCORONAZIONE DI POPPEA. Calvalli composed L'ORMINDO and LA CALISTO. Purcell composed DIDO and AENEAS in 1684. Rameau composed HIPPOLLYTE of ARTICLE and CASTOR et POLLUX. HANDEL composed GIULIO CESORE (1723-1724). TAMERLAND (1724-1731), RODELINIDA (1725), ORLANDO (1733), ARIODANTE (1735), ALCINA (1735), SERSE (1738) and SEMELE in 1744.

During the Baroque Era Alessandro Scarlatti was credited with the invention of the da capo aria. He was well known for his keyboard effects like his son, Domencico. Henadel had many of his operas performed at the Kings' Theatre in London, designed by John Vanbrugh. The only surviving part of Pergalesi's opera 11 PRIGIONIERO SUPERBO, was a two act Intermezzo still being performed (first edition, 1752).

During the classical Era in mid-18th-19th centuries featured operas were Gluck's operas ORFEDEN EURIDICE (1762), ALCESTE (1766-1767), IPHIGENIE en AULIEDE (1774), ARMIDE (1776-1777), and IPHIGENTE en TAURIDE (1778). Mozart composed IDOMENEDO (1780-1781), DIE ENTFUHRUNG AUS DEM SERAIL (1781-1782), LE NOZZE DIFIGARO, II DISSSOLLUTIO PUNITO, OSSIA II DON GIOVANNI, COSI FANTUTTE (1789), DIE ZAUBER FLOTE (1790-1791), and LA CLEMENZA DI TIATO in 1791). Beethoven composed FIDELTIO in (1805-1814).

Gioachino Rosini (1792-1868) was born in Pesaro, an Italian town, which holds an annual opera festival bearing his name. He wrote operas such as DEMETRIO e POLIBIO in 1806 and LACAMBILE DI MATRIMONIO (The Bill Of Marriage) which was quite successful and has occasionally been revived. Rossini composed THE BARBER OF SEVILLE in 1816. Another opera he composed is LA CENERENTOLA OSSIA LA BONTA IN RON FO (Cinderella) or Goodness Triumphs in 1817). LA CENERENTOLA is a modern production at the annual Rossini Opera Festival in Pesaro.

Gaetano Donizeti (1797-1848) composed a large body of orchestral chamber, choral and vocal music. He wrote 65 operas. He was born in Bergamo. His talent was recognized early and he studied in his home town and in Bologna with some of the best teachers in Italy. There are engravings of the garden at Windsor Castle for a set design for Donezetti's ANNA BOLENA.

Luciano Pavarotti, a well known tenor in the 20th century, performed in L'ELISIR D'AMORE (The Elixir of Love) in 1932. Luciano Pavarotti is one of the famous tenors of our modern times.

Donizetti's last major successful opera was DON PASQUALE in 1834 in the 19th Century. Gabriel Bacquier as Dr. Malatesta and Germain Evans played major roles in DON PASQUALE. He also composed LUEEZIA BORGIA and LA SCALA in Milan, Italy.

Vincenzo Bellini (1801-1835) was the last born of the three major bel canto composers. He died at age 33. Bellini was born in Catalina in Sicily, the oldest of seven children. He had his earliest musical training education from his father and his grandfather, both of whom were musicians. At 18, Bellini entered the San Sebastiano Conservatory in Naples. Niccolo Zingarelli was a composer and violinist, who introduced him to the music of the old Neapolitan Company and also of Hayden and Mozart.

Bellini traveled to England to continue his musical career. He met Chopin and German poet Heinrich Heine. He heard performances of Beethoven's orchestral music, which strongly impressed him. He composed I CAPULETIIMONTECCHT (The Capulets and Montagues, in 1830 and LA SONNABULA (The Sleepwalker) in 1831. He also wrote NORMA in 1831 and I PURITANI (The Puritans) in 1834-1835. Bellini wrote 10 operas. Beverly Sills sang the lead in I PURITANI as Elvira in 1977.

Puccini, who was from Italy, became famous for his opera LA BOHEME, which has been a very successful opera. Giuseppe Verdi (1813-1901) composed LA TRAVIATA, AIDA and RIGELETTO, which are very successful operas we see and hear even today at opera houses. Placido Domingo, Jose Carreras and Luciano Pavarotti, famous tenors, have sung lead parts in Puccini and Verdi's operas. The Welshman Bryn Terfel was in the title-role of Verdi's FALSTAFF in London in 2002.

Carl Maria von Weber composed DER FREISCHUTZ (The Freeshooter in (1817-1821). This opera, with its strong German folk influence, was an immediate success. Richard Wagner (1813-1883) composed operas such as LOHENGRIN, TANNHAUSER and THE SONG CONTEST on the WAERTBURG in 1843-1845, which all became well known and successful.

The most famous Wotan of the 20th Century Hares Hotter in DAS RHEINGOLD in London in 1957, composed the last opera and PARIFAL in 1865. George Bizet (1838-1875) wrote CARMEN, a very famous opera. Pyatr Tchaikovsky (18440-1893) composed operas such as EUGENE ONEGIN (1877-1878) and THE QUEEN OF SPADES (1890). Rimsky Korsakov composed THE GOLDEN COCKEREL and THE SNOW MAIDEN, which became famous operas. Rimsky-Korsakov was the youngest of a group of five Russian composers known as the "Mighty Handful." The other opera composers were Balokirev, Cui, Borodin and Musorgsky.

The late romantics who featured operas are Mascogani's

CAVALLERIA RUSTICANA (1888-1889), Leoncavallo's CPAGLIACCO (1892), Leoncavallo's PAGLICACCO (1892), Puccini's MANON LESCAUT (1882-1892), LA BOHEME (1893-1895), TOSCAUI (1896-1899) and MADAME BUTTERFLY in 1901-1906). Humperdinck composed HANSEL UND GRETEL. Straus composed SALOME, ELEKTRA, DEER ROSENKAVALIER, ARIADE AUFNAXOS, ARABELLA and CAPPRICIO. Debussy composed PELLEAS ET MELISANDE. JONACEK composed JENUFA, KATYAKABANOVA, THE CUNNING LITTLE VIXEN and MAKROPULOS AFFAIR.

Operas are still being written in modern times. Many people still attend operas.

FORTY-THREE

OCEANS AND SEAS ON EARTH

70 percent of the Earth's surface is covered with oceans and seas. Life on Earth originated in the oceans over 3.5 billion years ago, eventually creating our oxygen-rich atmosphere. The oceans regulate our climate and stabilize the conditions for life. Much is yet to be learned about our oceans. OCEANS: AN ILLUSTRATED REFERENCE is a wonderful designed volume which will introduce you to a fascinating and complex world and you will better understand the role that the oceans play in our lives.

Humans are changing the Earth. The upcoming century of ocean exploration will be as eventful and innovative as the last. From the dawn of history the ocean has served as a hunting ground for fishermen and a highway for transportation and trade. It has offered adventure and challenge to explorers and scientists, as well as providing the battlefield for a long pageant of human adventures.

The sheer immensity of the oceans reaches many places and its unfathomable depths have been a source of wonderment and the ocean's beauty and vitality have impressed humanity.

Earth is an ocean planet and the oceans are the last great frontier for human endeavor. Mankind should consider the protection of the water system known as rivers, lakes, seas and oceans. Oil spills should be avoided.

Earth had its origins some 3.5 billion years ago in the primeval ocean that covered the surface of the planet. Countless legions of organisms have lived and perished in the long process of evolution since those first tiny cells stirred. The living world is one of constant evolution and change, of great profusion and opportunism.

The Earth is in continual motion. Ocean crust is continually created and destroyed. Mountains rise from the sea, slowly erode and are once again returned as dust to the ocean basins, only to rise again. Patterns of change are forever cyclic, although the timescales vary and the past is never exactly repeated. The cycle of rocks, of sea level and of climate are all inextricably linked to the oceans and to life. Ocean space is the last great frontier on the planet. Tectonic plates move under the oceans. Tectonic plates effect the movement and temperature of the ocean.

Major oceans on Earth are the Pacific Ocean, the Atlantic Ocean, The Indian Ocean, Arctic Ocean and Antarctic Ocean. Different seas are the Barents Sea, Norwegian Sea, Mediterranean Sea, Black Sea, Labrador Sea, Caribbean Sea, Aegean Sea, and Sea of Mermara, Chukchi Sea, Beaufort Sea, Labrador Sea, Kara Sea, Amundsen Sea and Ross Sea, etc.

There are many more seas than there are oceans. The seas are much smaller than the oceans. In our solar system the Earth has much more water than the other planets. We need to keep our water clean in order to survive. We depend on water in order to continue to exist.

FORTY-FOUR

THE PERSIAN CULTURE

"The origins of the Persian people and the stages led to the creation of the first ancient world empire shrouded in mystery," said Pierre Briant, who studied about the Persian culture. We remain uninformed about the first centuries of Persian history between about 1000 and 600 BC.

The Persian founder Cyrus the great, became king of Persia around 557 BC. He was the son of Cambyses I and the grandson of Cyrus both of whom reigned over the country of Anshon, in the heart of the region which would take the name of Persia (Parsa). The Persians maintained a specific relationship with the Medes, both on a cultural and a political level.

Cyrus the Great (557-530 BC) and his army in 550 BC conquered Ecbatana and the Median Kingdom. Four years later Sardis, the kingdom of Lydia and Asia Minor, was in 539 BC. Cyrus defeated the Babylonian King Neabonidus and entered Babylon. After these conquests all the kings and rulers of the fertile crescent came to bow before their new master at the same time Cyrus authorized the Jews he exiled to Babylon since 587 BC to return to Jerusalem and rebuild the temple of Yahweh.

Meanwhile, Cyrus the Great may have launched an expedition across the Iranian plateau into Central Asia as far as Bactria-Soddiana, where he established a series of forts on the left bank of the River

Jaxartes (Syr Darya) which would be regarded as the northern border of the empire

The once small kingdom of Persia had become the center of an impressive empire. From this point on the Empire stretched from the Syr Darya to the first cataract of the Nile and from Samakand to the Mediterranean.

It was in 522-520 BC that the empire had its first serious crisis. It wasn't destroyed by it. The episode known by Herodotus explained that Darius himself gave on the cliff at Bisitun who endangered both the dynamic line and Persian imperial domination. Gautama of Darius seized power in Persia with a counter-attack to remove the rivals.

During the reign of Darius (522-486 BC) the empire reached its peak. In 513 BC Darius led his armies into Europe. He conquered the western coast of the Euxine Sea (The Black Sea). He crossed the River Danube (Istras) in pursuit of the Scythian armies. He left a strong army in Europe charged to annex Thrasce and Macedonia. When he stayed in Saris an Achaemeniala royal currency, the daric gold coin and (silver coin) had a warrior king stamped on them. By 490 BC the empire extended from the Indus to the Balkans.

The construction of the largest royal residence at Susa and Perspolis is the most brilliant testimony to Persian imperial power. Gold and silver tablets expressed Darius' thoughts. However, Persia was not a monarchy of constitutional type. The Achaemenid king was not only the "King of Persia." He was the intermediary between the Persian gods and the population of his country, but also the "king of kings", the king of lands which extends so far. The questioning of dynamic power often had repercussions in various subject countries.

The language of the rulers, Old Persian, belongs to the Indo-European family, whose members include language spoken from India (ancient Sanscript, modern Hindi and others), to Europe (ancient Latin and Greek, modern Romans, Germans and Slavic languages. Indo-Iranian languages are a subgroup of Indo-Iranian. The ancient written Iranian languages are Old Persian, Avestan (the language of the Zoroastrian scriptures and Pahlavi (the language of the Sassanian inscriptions. Modern Iranian languages include modern Persian (Farsi, the indirect descendant of the language of the Achaermenid inscriptions, Kurdish, Pashto and others).

Much of the common vocabulary of Old Persian is easily

recognizable from other Indo-European languages such as Old Persian, Latin, German and English. Use of languages determines how well different Persians were able to communicate effectively. Elamite has been the primary language of successive ancient kingdoms in territories of Western Iran. The third language of the trilingual inscriptions is a Babylonian dialect of Akkadian, a Semitic language which relates to Hebrew, Arabic and others. Akkadian texts were written in Mesopotamia as early as about 2400 BC and continued to be written until about AD 75. A few Achaemenid inscriptions also have versions in Egyptian and Aramaic, and it was also a written language used by Egypt, Babylonia and Persia. Aramaic is a northwest Semitic language related to Hebrew and Phoenician, spoken in Syria and northern Mesopotamia at the end of the second millennium BC around 950 BC.

Mohammed Ali, a religious prophet, changed the Middle East when he established the Moslem religion. Many Middle Eastern people believed in the Moslem religion. Mohammed developed a religious philosophy in which his followers were expected to kneel five times a day to pray to Allah. For one month a year Moslems are expected to experience lent. Women wear veils over their faces in order not to be seen by men. They are covered from head to their toes so men will not gaze at them for sexual purposes. Moslems must wash themselves before they pray. Moslems are expected to repent in order to prepare to overcome worldly temptations.

The Persian Culture flourished especially in Baghdad, where beautiful palaces and gardens were built. However, the Mongols invaded Iraq and took over this country. The Arabians also invaded Iraq and Iran. This changed life in Persia. Invaders dominated Persia. The Persians had to do what their invaders wanted them to do for centuries.

Oil was discovered around 1905 in Persia. The English came to Iran to promote oil refineries. Winston Churchill from England felt the oil was far more valuable than coal. Oil was used as petroleum in cars. The Iranians and Iraqis prospered by doing business with the English regarding the use of oil. Eventually Americans established business deals with the Middle East by purchasing oil from Iraq, Iran and Amorite countries.

The majority of Middle Easterners are Moslems. There are Shiites and Kurds, as well. There have been wars in Iraq, Afghanistan, Egypt and Syria because of political differences and attitudes about distribution of oil. America is trying to establish democracy in the Middle East. People in Iraq and Afghanistan are allowed to vote today. This is a positive step for these people.

FORTY-FIVE

IMAGINE IF YOU COULD FLY

Imagine if you could fly! You would be able to travel to many places and look down to the Earth to observe the landscape, oceans, rivers, lakes, creeks and mountainsides. You would be free to go to almost every place you wanted to see.

Birds fly freely to faraway places in order to live in warmer climates. If you could fly you could enjoy flying to the South Sea Islands of Tahiti, Tonga, The Philippine Islands, Fiji, New Guinea, New Zealand, Guam, Papua New Guinea, Easter Island and more. You could fly to Hawaii in the Northern Pacific and the Virgin Islands and other Caribbean Islands in the West Indies of the Northern Hemisphere.

Feel the wind on your wings as you move across the sky through clouds and mist. Look at curving mountains with high slopes as you fly high in the sky. The cool breeze will keep you alert. Become aware of birds flying nearby as you fly by. You can fly with the birds and watch how they move their wings.

The faster you fly the freer you will feel. You will reach your destination much sooner when you fly. Human beings are not designed to fly. They do not have wings when they are born. Human beings are grounded as a rule unless they wear man made wings that are run by electricity. To imagine what it is like to fly is not enough.

Batman and Superman have been seen flying high in the sky in movies. They are the heroes in movies. They are able to fly swiftly and fly to far away places. They help people in trouble.

People wish they could fly. They want to fly like birds so they can feel freer. People want to go beyond the horizon to discover faraway places.

FORTY-SIX

DECORATE YOUR HOME
WITH A CHRISTMAS TREE

Christmas is a very special time of the year. During this festive time of the year many people decorate their homes with Christmas trees. They go out to find the best tree available. Once a pine tree is selected it is brought home to be placed in a central place in their home.

Christmas trees are decorated so they look festive and colorful. Electric bulbs, hanging ornaments, candy sticks, sparkling glitter, immature dolls and long strands of colorful, hanging material are spread around the Christmas tree. A gold star or angel is hung at the top of the Christmas tree. White wrapping paper is wrapped around the base of the Christmas tree.

Each Christmas tree looks decorative and cheerful especially after it has been decorated. Family members gaze at the Christmas tree to enjoy its beauty and to smell its fragrance. Christmas gifts are placed under the Christmas tree.

Homes without decorated Christmas trees at Christmas time lack the Christmas spirit which makes Christmas very special. So, be sure to decorate your home with a Christmas tree.

FORTY-SEVEN
BE THANKFUL

Be thankful you are alive. Be grateful for everything you receive on a daily basis. Thankfulness can help you realize the importance of helping others and by giving to others. Even if you receive very little, be grateful for the little you received.

Birthdays are a time to be grateful for being remembered and for receiving birthday cards and gifts. At Christmas we usually receive Christmas cards and gifts. This is another time to be grateful. Thanksgiving Day and Easter time are festive times when we celebrate.

Be grateful when other people are friendly and helpful. Reach out to other people in return. They may be grateful for your help. Gratitude can go along way in restoring others as well as ourselves.

Starving people need food and they also need shelter as well as protection. When you give food, clothing and provide shelter to impoverished people they usually are thankful.

Thank God for loving you and protecting you. God provides fruits, vegetables, grain, sunshine and fresh air so we can survive on the Earth. We can learn to plant fruit seeds and vegetable gardens so we can have enough to eat. There is fresh water in streams, rivers, lakes and underground waterways so that we have enough water. Fresh air refreshes us as well.

So, be thankful to God for providing enough natural resources so that you can survive. You have the opportunity to have a healthy, happy life.

FORTY-EIGHT

MASSAGE TECHNIQUES

Massage treatments are helpful to heal damaged muscles and bones. Hand massages are used to stimulate muscles, joints and other body tissue. Massage therapists circulate the blood stream as they massage muscles. Circulated blood brings life and energy to the muscles and nervous system. With more positive energy circulating in specific areas of the body, pressure and pain can be released in a person's body.

People with back trouble, joint pains, aching bones and body muscles have been helped by chiropractors. They have regular, massage treatments in order to overcome backaches, painful joints, sore muscles and other body tissues. Massage therapy is an effective way to relax and overcome pain and stress. Be sure to select a chiropractor or massage therapist who knows how to massage you properly. Ask relatives and friends about good chiropractors and massage therapists to contact.

FORTY-NINE
CHORAL PRESENTATIONS

Choral presentations are presented with five part harmony. There are sopranos, mezzo-sopranos, altos, tenors and baritones. Each harmony stands close together. All five parts learn to harmonize together. They must keep accurate harmony and rhythm.

Choral groups sing madrigal songs, classical songs, folk songs, religious songs and Broadway songs. Choral arrangements with accompliments are magnificent to listen to.

Names of choral music are The Holy City, Hallelujah Halleluiah, Twelve Days of Christmas, Sing We And Chant It, Love Divine, All Love Excelling, Sweet Hour Of Prayer, Blest Be The Tie That Binds, Holy, Holy! Holy! Lord God Almighty, Shall We Meet Beyond the River? Abide With Me and Hosanna In the Highest. More carols especially sung at Christmas are Here We Come a Caroling, Silent Night, The Holly And The Ivy, Winter Wonderland, Jingle Bells, O Christmas Tree, O Little town of Bethlehem, Hark! The Herald Angels Sing, Joy To The World and We Wish You a Merry Christmas.

Other popular songs that have been arranged for choral presentations are Memory, Moonglow, More, The Rainbow Connection, Unchained Melody, Unforgettable, Bridal Chorus, Deep River, Go Down Moses, In the Gloaming, Lead, Kindly Light, Lullaby, Nearer My God To Thee, Onward Christian Soldiers, Rock Of Ages, Silver Threads Among The Gold, Serenade, Sweet and Low and Whispering Hope.

More choral arrangements are Praise to the Almighty, The King of Creation. When Jesus Walked On Galilee, Faure-Crucifix, Gund O, Divine Redeemer, Ring Out Wild Bells, Tchaikovsky—The Lord Is My Shepherd and Mozart---O Lord On High.

Many more choral arrangements have been composed. Choral presentations take place at church, at community programs, at festivals, ceremonies and at choral concerts. Choral music is popular still. Many people attend choral presentations.

FIFTY

AT MIDSTREAM

Al and Alisha Armando enjoyed strolling near running streams. They went barefooted in cool, refreshing streams. They watched for rocks and pebbles as they continued walking downstream to avoid stepping on sharp objects in the moving water.

Finally, Al and Alisha approached midstream. The water was deeper and currents of water were moving swiftly to the center of the stream and then into different directions. Al and Alisha were in the deeper water which rose up higher and higher against their bodies. They were sopping wet. They both began to shiver in the deeper water.

Yet, Al and Alisha continued by floating in the cool stream. They moved against the cool, midstream water. Rippling currents of water splashed against them. They kept floating in the stream. They began to struggle against the currents. Alisha suddenly went under in the deep stream water because the currents were so strong.

Al noticed that Alisha had disappeared in the deep stream. He decided to search for her. He swam under the water to look for her. He kept looking for Alisha. The stream was dark at midstream. He couldn't see Alisha in the dark water. He kept looking for her.

Finally, Al came up for air. He took several, deep breaths. He went back down into the deep stream to search for Alisha. She eventually came up for air. Al swam over to her. He put her on his back and swam to shore. He laid Alisha out onto the embankment.

Al noticed Alisha was lying on the embankment helpless. She didn't seem to be breathing. He applied CPR techniques to help Alisha breathe better. He moved her arms up and down across her chest. Stream water oozed out of her mouth. She began to cough. More water came up. Finally, Alisha began to breathe again.

Alisha kept breathing more regularly. Al was glad Alisha was recovering from her ordeal in the stream. He thought she might drown if he hadn't found her in time. He put a dry towel around her shoulders and chest. He wanted Alisha to be warmer. Alisha was shivering because she had been in cool water long enough to become cold.

The sunshine began to warm Alisha up. Al also began to dry off and warm up. They lay on the grassy embankment to warm up and to recover from the deeper part of the midstream. They were grateful to be out of danger. Al spoke to Alisha. He said, "We better not step into the deeper water in the midstream ever again. I don't want anything to happen to you." Alisha looked at Al warmly and said, "You are right. I had a close call today. I was pulled into the swift current. Then I went under suddenly. I had a lot of difficulty coming up for air. I thought I would drown. Thank you for helping me out of the water. You saved my life."

Al looked at Alisha very warmly. He reached out to her and embraced her. Then he kissed her gently on her lips. They continued to lie there in the warm sunshine.

FIFTY-ONE

ORIGINAL POEMS

FASCINATING MOMENTS

Fascinating moments awaken me
I visualize adventures and see
Snow-capped mountains with glee
Waterfalls gleam with sun beams

Allured by chirping songbirds
Nature scenes are described in words
Pine and spruce forests vividly occur
Orange, calico cats wag tails and purr

Hike over hillsides and into valleys
Flowers and shrubs exist in alleys
Dancers gracefully move in ballets
Boats navigate in waterways without delay

Rainbows beam with multiple light
Red, orange, green, yellow sights
Splashing waves flow with might
Children fly beautiful, colorful kites

SUNRISE, SUNSET

Sunrise gleams in early morning time
Sunlight hues beam with designs
Pastel colors are so refined
Streaky shapes spread like lines

Sunsets so vivid rise near the horizon
Sheep, cattle, horses graze with bisons
Sunsets spread across the night sky
Clusters of puffy clouds move by

Sunrises, sunsets, often come and go
Bright colors emanate and glow
Creative patterns emerge and flow
Nature's designs spread like petals of a rose

Begin each morning viewing a vivid sunrise
Observe how the sun moves the sky
End the day with a sunset
Walk on a pristine beach with someone you have met.

PARADISE

Paradise is a wonderland of peace
Ambrosia and bliss, a spiritual feast

Enlightenment, joy and love abide
Mystic sounds, sights and rolling ebb tides

Higher dimensions emerge within
Paradise enlightens one's soul without sin

FIFTY-TWO

TRAVELING ON
AN AMTRAK TRAIN

Sara Williamson, a middle aged, auburn hair woman, dressed in conservative clothes, was traveling on an Amtrak train from Minnesota to Albany, New York in 1985. She sat near big window and she was able to observe scenery while she traveled. Sara noticed pine, spruce, aspen, birch and sycamore trees growing in forests or groves. The Amtrak train passed many groves. The Amtrak passed many meadows and fields of flowers, wild flowers, shrubs, bushes as well as streams, creeks, lakes, and even traveled near rivers. She felt sunlight coming through the windows.

Several passengers were headed to New York. Sara decided to become acquainted with some of these passengers. She met a mother and her two children. The mother was in her early thirties. Her two daughters were 7 and years old. Sara became interested in knowing the two girls as well as their mother. She introduced herself to them. Sara asked, "Have you traveled on Amtrak before? The nine year old girl replied, "No. This is my first train ride." Sara said, "Where are you traveling to?" The nine year old girl answered, "We are going to New York City." Sara smiled at her. Sara asked, "What is your name?" The girl replied, "My name is Judy. This is my mother, Eileen and my sister, Alice."

Eileen, the mother spoke, "We are going to New York City to visit relatives. I haven't been to New York City for years." Sara smiled at Eileen and her two girls. The train continued moving over one hundred miles an hour toward New York City. Eileen and her girls were sitting around a table. The girls were playing scrabble. Later, they played checkers. They also looked at the view from the window.

Sara continued to observe the girls playing games. There were other tables where passengers were playing cards. Some passengers were drinking sodas and eating snacks. The Amtrak train continued moving swiftly on the track towards New York City.

Lunch was served at noon time on the train. Passengers went to the dining car to eat their lunch. Waiters brought roasted lamb, curried rice, steamed vegetables, sourdough bread, butter, tea or coffee and tapioca pudding. Children were served milk. Passengers ate their lunch while they watched scenery when they looked out the windows.

Sara had an opportunity to meet more passengers while she ate lunch. She was enjoying the train trip. She had already traveled over one hundred and fifty miles. The train was approximately one hundred miles away from New York City. The train continued to go one hundred miles an hour. It would arrive on time in New York City.

After lunch, Sara and the other passengers walked back to their train compartments. They sat down where they had been sitting. Some luggage was near passenger seats. Sara thought about her experiences on the train. She looked forward to arriving in New York City. Sara said good bye to passengers she met on the Amtrak train.

The Amtrak stopped at New York City Amtrak Station at 11:30 p.m. Sara collected her luggage and stepped off the Amtrak train into the Amtrak station. She flagged down a taxi. A taxi driver stepped out of his taxi. He put Sara's luggage in his taxi. When Sara was in the taxi he asked where she wanted to go. Sara told the taxi driver to take her to the Holiday Inn on 7th Street. Sara was glad she traveled on the Amtrak train all the way to New York City. After she enjoyed the sights, cultural events and restaurants in New York City she planned to take an Amtrak train to Albany, New York to visit relatives. She felt comfortable traveling by Amtrak train. When she had planned to return, she took an Amtrak train to Minnesota

FIFTY-THREE
GALACTIC AWARENESS

During the 20th and 21st centuries more people are becoming conscious of galactic awareness. UFOs have been sited over major cities around the world. Beings from outer space have been witnessed on Earth. People are becoming much more open and accepting of celestial beings.

Photographs, newspaper and magazine articles, films and television programs have been presented about outer space and about our Universe and Cosmos. People are developing much more understanding and perception about our solar system, different constellations and galaxies.

Erich Von Daniken, George Adamski, Billy Mier, Bill Birnes, Steven Hawking and many other investigators have gathered evidence about UFOs, aliens and expressed their viewpoints about our Universe and solar system, Erich Von Daniken has traveled to the Andes Mountains in South America to observe the Naska Lines which are bird and insect designs. He thought this was an ancient air strip for ancient astronauts. He collected alien objects and photographed drawings of outer space beings in spacesuits. Some outer space beings were in flying objects called "chariots" and flying saucers. Von Daniken observed flying objects from outer space shown over Bethlehem during Jesus' birth. Space aliens wore space helmets and space suits, which are revealed in many paintings and drawings. Erich Von Daniken believes ancient astronauts came to Earth millions of years ago.

George Adamski wrote books about space beings and flying saucers in the 1950s. He claimed he met beings from Venus, Mars and Jupiter, who had contacted him. He went into the Mojave Desert to encounter a Venusian who showed Adamski a silver colored flying saucer. Adamski was shown inside this flying saucer. Adamski wrote INSIDE THE FLYING SAUCER. He claims he was taken to Venus. The celestial beings were friendly and seemed advanced according to Adamski's description.

Bill Birnes has observed UFOs for many years. He has documented information and filmed UFOs moving in our atmosphere. Some outer space objects move in groups. Flying saucers have been filmed which are circular as well as cigar shaped. Bill Birnes has talked about Area 51 as well as the Roswell location. He claims spaceships landed on Earth because they ran out of fuel. Space men, who were short, with large eyes, were found. These dead outer space aliens were collected and taken into a hanger along with their space crafts to be examined. This 1947 Roswell incident was concealed by the American government for years from the American public.

Steven Hawking, who has a Ph.D in Aerospace and Physics, claims black holes exist in many galaxies. Black holes are at the very center of expanding galaxies. Black holes suck in everything around them because they create a strong vortex of energy. Recently, Steven Hawking has developed a theory about an invisible, parallel universe which is a duplicate of the physical universe. Hawking has developed theories about how the Universe expands. He described dying suns and their effect on solar systems and galaxies.

I believe that celestial beings came from The Pleiades millions of years ago to live on Earth on ancient Lemuria and Atlantis. Today underwater colonies of aliens dwell in our oceans. Ancient outer space astronauts landed on Earth and formed our ancient civilizations in Lemuria, Atlantis, Sumeria, Babylon, China, India and other places. Galactic awareness is continuing to occur in the world.

FIFTY FOUR

USING DIFFERENT PENS AND PENCILS

Different pens and pencils are used in specific ways. Some pens are used mainly to write letters, essays and reports. The ink in pens may be permanent ink or waterproof ink. Other ink may be washable when it smears. It may be erased. Red, blue, black, purple and green colored ink may be used to write with. Ink must be produced with dyes and chemicals produced into liquids.

Pencils are also used to write with. Big, thick, wooden pencils are used by primary grades. Regular sized pencils are used by older children. The lead in pencils can be erased. Pencils are very useful. Drawing pencils have more charcoal colors so that drawings look more artistic. Drawing pencils are used for shading and contrast created in different pictures.

Regular Number 1, 2 and 3 pencils are generally used to do daily school work in elementary schools and high schools around the world. Pencils are used in Western societies today. Feather pens are no longer used in modern civilizations. Colored pencils are used to color in drawings and illustrations.

Kado pens are used to make poster drawings, poster letters, on black cards, signs and bulletin boards.

Very expensive ink pens usually last much longer than ordinary pens. Pens packaged in tens or twelve pens are usually inexpensive pens which do not last very long. Quality pens have one or two in a package.

Pencils may be packaged 1, 2 or 3 in a container. Mechanical pencils in which lead is put into metal pencils are used. Many people use metal pencils with lead added inside the pencils.

There are many pencil and pens used to write and draw with. Each pen or pencil is useful.

FIFTY-FIVE

MARVELS AND WONDERS

Marvels and wonders exist in the world. The marvels of spring flowers are magnificent. Fragrant aromas permeate the air. Splendid views of rainbows light up the sky. Mountaintops are covered with snow and they reach to the sky.

Azure blue skies reflect in ponds, lakes, rivers and oceans. Sunsets gleam in lagoons. Birds flock overhead and spread their wings. Their wings may glitter in the sunlight. Thousands of pink flamingos cluster closely together to create a pink glow of fluttering wings. Wonders exist in Nature. Doves coo. Turtles move slowly in their shells. Hummingbirds produce swift, wing movements

Diamonds sparkle in the light. Rhythmic waves flow back and forth to shore. Billions of grains of sand exist at beaches. Seagulls, herons and pelicans wander about near the oceans.

Glance at brilliant crimson sunsets. Awaken at sunrise to a new day of vivid colors spreading across the morning sky. Enjoy verdant green forests and meadows. Marvel at Blue Jays, meadowlarks, robins, flinches, whippoorwills and owls moving about in forests and plains. Tall grass with sunflowers growing in fields create colorful views.

Marvels and wonders exist in the Universe. Swirling planets follow orbits about our sun. Our sun moves around in our galaxy. Blue, white, yellow, violet, red and green colors are seen in our Universe. Unique geometric designs exist throughout the cosmos lighting up outer space.

NONFICTION

FIFTY-SIX

COBBLESTONE ROADS
AND STREETS

Cobblestone roads have been made in Europe and America especially in olden times. Narrow streets as well as wider streets have been carefully built with individual cobblestones placed close together.

Larger, thick, smooth stones have been artistically placed in the ground one at a time. Stones are different colors such as tan, brown, green and red. Bricks which are manmade are also used to build roads and pathways.

Cobblestone roads are pleasant to look at. They have a unique style. Many cobblestone streets have been built in villages and small towns throughout Europe. Early Americans built cobblestone and brick streets.

Early Romans built stone streets in their cities and countryside. Many stone streets stretched for many miles from one town to another. Cobblestone roads were started by ancient civilizations in Babylonia, Egypt, Sumeria as well as ancient Rome and Greece.

Cobblestone streets and roads are still being built in modern times because they are unique and artistic.

FIFTY-SEVEN

BE CHARITABLE

A giving person is charitable. Those individuals who donate money, food and other belongings usually care about other people. They are willing to help needy people, who need food, clothing and shelter. Kindly deeds such as transporting homeless people to care centers, shelters and community services helps underprivileged individuals survive. Every charitable action can serve others in dire need.

Becky Hillman was a charitable person. She observed many homeless, needy people standing in the streets downtown and near major streets and freeways. She gave money to homeless people. She donated food to the food banks in town. She was deeply concerned about people who slept outside and who had no employment. She wondered why homeless people were not provided with places to live. Becky told homeless people about free luncheons at churches in town.

Becky decided to provide a shelter for homeless people. She located a big, old house in the older part of town. There were ten bedrooms in this old house. Becky decided to fix up this old house. She hired friends to restore the floors, walls, ceilings and doors throughout the house. Then she helped to repaint each room. The windows were remodeled. The roof was rebuilt with new wood and shingles. The outside of the big house was repainted a cheerful yellow with green trim.

Once the house was restored Becky added attractive wall-to-wall carpeting. Then, she looked for attractive, used furniture to put in each room. She bought double bunk beds for some more homeless people to stay in the house. Four double bunk beds were placed in each bedroom for homeless people to sleep in.

Eight people could sleep in each bedroom. So, this meant that 80 individuals could stay at this new shelter because there were ten bedrooms. Becky cooked hot meals twice a day to provide nutritional food for many homeless occupants at the shelter. She also became acquainted with many of those individuals who stayed at the shelter.

Homeless occupants were encouraged to help clean up in this big, old house. Some homeless individuals volunteered to help cook meals. They also helped to serve the meals during the lunch and dinner meals. This helped homeless individuals feel a sense of responsibility and belonging. Occupants also emptied the garbage, swept and mopped floors. They dusted and washed daily laundry.

Becky Hillman focused on self responsibility, personal hygiene as well as respectful conduct in the big, old house. As time went by her house for the homeless people became an ideal place for needy, homeless people to stay. Some of the homeless people had more incentive to seek employment after doing chores at the big old house. They came back to tell Becky about how their lives had changed because they received jobs. Becky had given them hope and understanding. More and more homeless people came to this shelter through the years because they heard this was the best shelter in the whole regional area.

FIFTY-EIGHT

AVOID UNNECESSARY TOXINS

Pure spring water cleanses and helps us remain healthy. Spring water is much safer and healthier for human beings to drink. Chlorine is put in tap water. Chlorine is poisonous.

Our bodies are exposed to bacteria. We are exposed to bacteria every day. We strengthen our immune system by developing natural immunities to harmful bacteria.

Kevin Trudeau has a reverse osmosis unit in his house. The water in his house is filtered. He uses a distiller to get rid of the energetic memory attached to the water. He drinks bottled water when he travels. He does not drink water which is filtered or purified.

Cholesterol is not the cause of heart disease. There are people with 600 cholesterol counts that have absolutely no arteriosterosis, no blockage as well as no heart diseases. There are people with cholesterol counts of 100 who have massive blockages and are dropping dead from heart attacks and need triple bypass-surgeries. The amount of cholesterol in your blood is not the problem. The problem occurs when the cholesterol attaches itself to the artery, thus clogging the artery and restricting the blood flow and what causes the cholesterol to attach itself to the artery. Cholesterol attaches itself to damaged arteries.

Chlorinated water which people drink scars arteries. Cholesterol attaches to scarred arteries. Hydrogenated oils or trans fats. These trans fats scar the arteries, causing disease and arteriosclerosis. Homogenized dairy products allow fat products. And is not natural. It is man-made. The homogenization process causes scarring which is in homogenized milk, margarine and cheese.

Chlorine and fluoride are two main poisons that are in our water. Remember that coffee, Lipton tea, sodas and alcohol are manmade. So, these drinks have chemicals. They are harmful. You should purchase a juice machine and use organic fruits and vegetables to produce organic juices.

Air fresheners contain deadly poisons in the air. These poisons kill off the receptors in your nose so you cannot smell the offending odor any more. They don't eliminate odors. They eliminate your ability to smell odors. Toxins get into our body through our skin. Everything you put on your skin gets into your bloodstream. Common ingredients in sunscreens cause cancer. The more sunscreen used causes skin cancers. Underarm deodorants and antiperspirants contain deadly chemicals that many people believe to be a major cause of breast cancer in women. "If you can't eat it do not put it on your skin," said Kevin Trudeau.

We need to take care of our eyes and ears. The major form of toxins that come in through the eyes are images that cause bad emotions. People are exposed to thousands of negative images. Negative images cause one's eyes to become blurry.

Sounds are vibrations and frequencies which affect our ears. Our ears can become degenerated. Certain harsh music can damage our ears. We need to listen to relaxing music and avoid loud, sharp sounds which can harm our ears.

Sources of unnatural, electromagnetic energy bombard our bodies everyday such as satellites, cell phone towers, cell phones, high tension, power lines, computers, televisions and radios. Fluorescent lights, microwave ovens and even people emit electromagnetic energy.

Another dynamic relating to electromagnetic energy is ions. There are positive and negative ions. Positively charged ions have an adverse effect on the body. Negatively charged ions have a positive health enhancing effect on the body. Wind blowing through trees emits wonderful negative ions. People feel better in a forest and when they are in the fresh air.

Common things which slow the elimination process are antibiotics, lotions and creams as well as lotions and creams and lack of body movements. We eliminate body toxins through our nose, mouth, the urinary tract, the colon and the skin.

FIFTY-NINE

ABOUT LAURA INGLES WILDER

Laura Ingalls Wilder was a well known American author in the prairie and Big Woods. Her parents, Pa and Ma Ingalls had moved to this wilderness land to build a log cabin house. The Big Woods was a way station on a long and restless journey West. Trees were chopped down to produce enough logs to build the little house on the prairie.

Nights dropped thirty-five and even forty degrees below zero. The wind blew swiftly. Snow fell during late autumn and in winter months. Laura's Pa was born January 10, 1836 and he was named Charles Philip Ingalls. He had Yankee blood and a hard sense of discipline. Charles father, Langford Ingalls was born in Canada. His roots reached back to New Hampshire and his wife's to Vermont. Charles Mather came from a French family several generations back.

Laura Ingalls was named after her grandmother with the name Laura. Laura's Pa grew up in lumber country. Her Pa had Big Woods to roam free in. Laura's Pa pretended to be a mighty hunter on the watch for prowling bears and wolves as well as panthers.

The Fox River was winding down from Wisconsin through woods of oak, elm and hickory beneath these trees and out along the edges of the bright prairie, wild raspberries and gooseberries grew in large quantities. There were strawberries and wild blackberries as well as hazelnuts, walnuts, butternuts and hazelnuts. Prairies were covered with tall blue grass with flowers such as hyacinth, indigo and shooting stars, cinquefoil and paintbrush. The grasses are called giant bluestem described in LAURA—THE LIFE OF LAURA INGALLS WILDER by Donald Zocher.

Laura Ingalls Mather was born in December in Milwaukee County, Wisconsin. Her family were Connecticut Yankees and they moved about. Laura never knew her Grandma Quiner or her Grandpa Quiner who died long before Laura was born. Grandma Quiner's name was Charlotte W. Tucker before she married Henry N. Quiner. They were married in New Haven, Connecticut in the spring of 1831. Laura's Ma may have been the first born in Wisconsin in the territory. Laura's Ma lost her father when she was seven. Grandma Quiner was left alone to raise Laura's Ma and her other children.

Grandpa and Grandma Ingalls found many Ingalls in Jefferson County in Wisconsin. Grandpa found a nice piece of land of 80 acres to settle down along the Oconomowoc River, only a few rods beyond the forms of the Quiners. Mr. Hallbrook, Grandpa and Grandma Ingalls paid for their land in 1853.

"Laura's mother helped take care of her sisters and brothers. She also had many chores around the farm. Laura's mother, Caroline Quiner Ingalls was beautiful. Her beauty was certainly more than skin deep. Pa could see that she was a good helpmate to share the long, hard days of his life. He could see her steadfast heart. She would follow where he went and would bear misfortune and privation to make a life together," said Laura Ingalls Wilder.

When Charles and Caroline Ingalls married in 1860 in Concord they moved West into prairie country surrounded by big woods. They built a log house and barn. They had three daughters and adopted a son after their fourth child died during infancy. Laura was the second child. She shared a bedroom loft with her older sister.

The Ingalls worked hard during the day. Charles Ingalls planted different crops on at heir farm. Caroline Ingalls cooked, cleaned house, fed the chickens, horses, dogs, cats and collected eggs. She taught her children to gather eggs and to feed the animals. Laura and her older sister learned to cook.

Charles enjoyed playing the violin in the evenings. He also told stories around the fireplace to his children. Laura learned a lot about storytelling from both of her parents. The Ingalls went on picnics near the river near their farm. Laura liked to fish with her father. She was close to both her parents.

The Ingalls drove to the nearest town to purchase important items at the store. Caroline Ingalls brought fresh eggs to the mercantile store to sell to the owners of the store. She bought fabric to make clothes for her family and herself.

Laura and her sisters and brother attended a one room schoolhouse in town. They had to walk to school and walk home after school. Laura learned the three Rs of reading, writing and arithmetic. Only one school marm taught in the one room schoolhouse. McDuffy Readers were used. Children who lived closest to the town attended the one room schoolhouse from Grade 1 through Grade 8.

Laura was enthusiastic about writing in a daily diary. She had learned to spell and write sentences in school. She described her life on the farm, at school, in town and other places. Laura wrote about her parents Charles and Caroline as well as her sisters and brothers. Laura described her daily experiences with her family.

Sibling rivalry occurred occasionally in the Ingalls household. Laura resented that a boy she was attracted to preferred her older sister Mary. Laura wanted the boy to like her and to become her special boyfriend when he showed far more interest in her older sister Mary. However, Mary finally told Laura that she wasn't interested in getting involved with this particular boy.

When Mary grew up, Laura discovered that Mary became blind. Mary eventually went to a school for the blind. Mary met another blind young man who fell in love with her. They were married happily. Mary had her eyes checked hoping she would overcome her blindness. Her husband eventually recovered his eye sight. He studied Law and became a successful lawyer. Mary learned Braille in order to read in Braille.

Laura grew up near the Wilders. She knew Almanzo, who she fell in love with. She attended barn dances with him and went on buggy rides with him in the countryside. Almanzo eventually proposed to Laura. She married Almanzo Wilder on August 25, 1885. They lived in the Wilder home in town. Laura taught at the one room schoolhouse when she was grown up before she was married to Almanzo.

Almonzo Wilder was a farmer. He planted crops and he harvested various crops. Laura began to write books during her married life. The television series THE LITTLE HOUSE ON THE PRAIRIE was based on the books of Laura Ingalls Wilder. This television series became popular during the 1960s on. Michael Landon, a well known actor, produced THE LITTLE HOUSE ON THE PRAIRIE.

Laura became a mother of her daughter named Rose. Laura wasn't sure she wanted to be a farmer's wife. What she did want, she couldn't say. ut in her heart she always called herself a pioneer girl. Even after many years, when she began her work on the Little House books, her first thought for a title was simply Pioneer Girl. She was used to being free and singing songs on the prairie and dreaming dreams that would come true.

Laura and Almanzo moved away from their farm after crops wilted and died. Almonzo had suffered from a stroke. He was unable to work a full day. Laura, Almonzo and their daughter moved in with Laura's father in town. Pa had moved away from his prairie farm.

Then Laura and Almanzo moved into a rented house near Ma and Pa Ingalls. Laura's sister, Mary had graduated from college. Her younger sister, Carrie was a young woman of twenty-two. She worked in the back of the newspaper office in town setting type. She was learning to be a printer. For a time, Laura's Pa had a little general store in the heart of town. He also sold insurance. He also did carpentry work.

Laura became a dressmaker with her old schoolmate, Hattie Dorchester who was also a dressmaker. Almanzo found odd jobs to do such as carpentry, driving teams and clerking in a store.

The years began to fly. Laura and Almanzo moved to a farm with forty acres. They grew hogs, sheep, Jersey cows and goats. Laura looked after Leghorn hens. She gathered eggs in the winter when none of her neighbors got them. Within two years Almanzo was able to put the farm on a paying basis. He grew corn, wheat and oats, grapes and other fruit.

Laura Ingall Wilders Pa died in 1902. She traveled back to be with him before his death. Then Laura went home to Almanzo. She was 35 years old. She was the farm wife she once thought she never could become. Laura continued to write in the evenings and other spare time. It took approximately 20 years for Laura Ingalls Wilders first book LITTLE HOUSE IN THE BIG WOOD to be published the way it was written. Laura Ingalls Wilder refused to let publishers control what was written in her books.

Laura Ingalls Wilder wrote a series of LITTLE HOUSE BOOKS.

She wrote LITTLE HOUSE IN THE BIG WOODS, LITTLE HOUSE ON THE PRAIRIE, FARMER BOY, ON THE BANKS OF PLUM CREEK, OLD TOWN IN THE GREEN GROVES, BY THE SHORES OF SILVER LAKE, THE LONG WINTER, THESE HAPPY GOLDEN YEARS, THE FIRST FOUR YEARS, ON THE WAY HOME, WEST FROM HOME, LITTLE HOUSE TRAVELER and THE LITTLE HOUSE CHRISTMAS TREASURY.

"Laura Ingalls Wilder reflects the best of pioneer days in America. She described the joys and hardships and complexities of pioneer life in the West," stated Donald Zochert who wrote LAURA—THE LIFE OF LAURA INGALLS WILDER.

SIXTY

WHO'S WHO IN
THE FILM INDUSTRY

Many famous actors and actresses work in the film industry. EDMUND GWENN, born in 1875 and died in 1959, began acting in the theater in 1895. He found success, becoming a favorite of George Bernard Shaw, who cast him in the first production of Man and Superman in 1902 and then in five more of his plays. Edmund Gwenn had star qualities such as he was an endearing character actor with comic timing. He played a whiskered old man with a smile. Gwenn played in PRIDE AND PREJUDICE, LASSIE COME HOME, BETWEEN TWO WORLDS, THEM and THE BEAST FROM 20,000 FATHOMS.

CHARLES COBERN, born in 1897 and died in 1961, was a stage actor, producer and director in Shakespeare drama. He was Southern gentleman able to do character parts and comedy roles. He treated the film industry as a lucrative retirement occupation. He was nominated as the best supporting actor in a romantic comedy THE MORE THE MERRIER. He acted as Sir Francis "Piggy" Beckman in GENTLELMEN PREFER BLONDES. Top film takes are THE STORY OF MANKIND, AROUND THE WORLD IN EIGHTY DAYS, MONKEY BUSINESS, THE LADY EVE And THE STORY OF ALEXANDER GRAHAM BELL.

LIONEL BARRYMORE was an artist, novelist, composer, director, producer and writer, a member of an acting dynasty, prolific cinematic output with endurance and determination. Barrymore acted in KEY LARGO, IT'S A WONDERFUL LIFE, YOUNG DR. KILDARE, YOU CAN'T TAKE IT WITH YOU, CAPTAINS COURAGEOUS, CAMILLE, DAVID COPPERFIELD, DINNER AT EIGHT, RASPUTIN AND THE EMPRESS, GRAND HOTEL, A FREE SOUL, THE MYSTERIOUS ISLAND and SADIE THOMPSON. He was born in 1878 and he died in 1954.

WILL ROGERS, born in 1879 and died in 1935, became a stage actor, radio personality, author, journalist and movie star. He became a cowboy humorist, trick roper and developed horsemanship. He was a warmhearted radio broadcaster and witty social commentator and influential newspaper columnist. He acted in LIFE BEGINS AT FORTY, JUDGE PRIEST, STATE FAIR, YOUNG AS YOU FEEL, A CONNECTICUT YANKEE, THEY HAD TO SEE PARIS, FRUITS OF FAITH, THE ROPIN' FOOL, ALMOST A HUSBAND and LAUGHING BILL HYDE.

W.C FIELDS was born in 1860 and died in 1946. His star qualities were virtuoso juggler, bulbous nose and muttering patter. He played the misanthrope, the malcontent and an egotist. He was a writing and comic genius. He acted in NEVER GIVE A SUCKER A CHANCE, MANY LITTLE CHICKADEES, YOU CAN'T CHEAT AN HONEST MAN, MAN AND THE FLYING TRAPESE, DAVID COPPERFIELD, IT'S A FIGHT, THE OLD FASHION WAY, YOU'RE TELLING ME! ALICE AND WONDERLAND, MILLION DOLLAR LEGS, FOOLS FOR LUCK, THE POTTERS, SALLY OF THE SAWDUST and HIS LORDSHIP DILEMMA.

DOUGLAS FAIRBANKS was born in 1883 and he died in 1939. His star qualities are his trademark moustache, flair for wearing costumes and capes, athletic daredevil, director, producer and writer. He invented the slyly self-parodic, action hero, setting the tone for a line of successors from Errol Flynn to Bruce Willis. He acted in THE PRIVATE LIFE OF DON JUAN, MR. ROBINSON CRUSOE, THE TAMING OF THE SHREW, THE IRON MASK, THE GAUCHO, THE BLACK PIRATE, DON Q, SONG OF ZORRO, THE THIEF OF BAGDAD, ROBIN HOOD, THE THREE MUSKETEERS MYSTERY OF THE LEAPING FROG and THE LAMB. Douglas Fairbanks established his own production company, the Douglas

Fairbanks Film Corporation. He established the United Artists Studio in 1919 together with Charles Chaplin, D.W. Griffith and Pickford Fairbanks who were also founders of the Academy of Motion Picture Arts and Sciences. He co-hosted with director William C. de Mille, the First Academy Awards ceremony in 1929.

WALTER HUSTON was born in 1884 and he died in 1950. He was head of an acting dynasty stagecraft. He was a versatile character who moved from Stetsons to suites. He was a producer and singer. He worked in vaudeville. Twenty years later he was a stage veteran. He went to Hollywood to appear in talking pictures. He acted in THE FURIES, THE TREASURE OF THE SIERRA MADRE, DUEL IN THE SUN, AND THEN THERE WERE NONE, THE OUTLAW, YANKEE DOODLE DANDY, THE DEVIL AND DANIEL WEBSTER, DODSWORTH, RHODES OF AFRICA, GARBRIEL OVER THE WHITE HOUSE, LAW AND ORDER, THE BEST OF THE CITY, THE STAR WITNESSS, THE CRIMINAL CODE, ABRAHAM LINCOLN and THE VIRGINIAN.

AL JOLSON was born in 1886 and he died in 1950. He was a singer, composer, whistler and electrifying entertainer. He sang tearjerkers, with any operatic twist and dramatic gestures. He sang hit songs. Al Jolson used blackface makeup. He sang My *Mammy* and *Sonny Boy*. He performed in THE JAZZ SINGER. He was the son of a rabbi who immigrated to Washington D.C. He performed ragtime to American troops. Al Jolson acted in SWANEE RIVER, ROSE OF WASHINGTON SQUARE, THE SINGING KID, GO INTO YOUR DANCE, VUNDERBARWONDER BAR, BIG BOY, MAMMY, SAY IT WITH SONGS, THE SINGING FOOL, THE JAZZ SINGER and MAMMY'S BOY.

CHARLIE CHAPLIN was born in 1889 and he died in 1977. He performed as a slapstick comedian, comic actor and film-maker. He was the biggest silent screen star. He was a director, studio head and was the cofounder of United Artists. He was a successful clown. He was one of the most popular entertainers of the twentieth century. Top films were A COUNTESS FROM HONG KONG, LIMELIGHT, MODERN TIMES, CITY LIGHTS, THE CIRCUS, THE GOLD RUSH, THE IDLE CLASS, THE KID, A DOG'S LIFE, THE IMMIGRANT, THE RINK, BEHIND THE SCREEN, THE COUNT, THE VAGABOND, THE FIREMAN, BURLESQUE ON CARMEN,

SHANGHAIED, THE TRAMP, IN THE PARK, A NIGHT OUT, HIS NEW JOB, HIS FAVORITE PAST TIME and KID AUTO RACES OF VENICE.

MAURICE CHEVALIER was born in 1888 and he died in 1972. His star qualities were his charm and sophistication. He was a singer, dancer and well known actor. Maurice was known for wearing a straw hat. He had a twinkle in his eyes. Chevalier started his career as an acrobat until he had an accident that forced him to turn to singing and acting. He starred in the film GIGI. He served in the French Army during World War I. He learned English which proved to be useful in his acting career. He eventually moved to Hollywood and worked at Paramount Pictures. He acted in MONKEYS GO HOME, I'D RATHER BE RICH, PANIC BUTTON, CAN-CAN, COUNT YOUR BLESSINGS, GIGI, LOVE IN THE AFTERNOON, MA POMME, THE MERRY WIDOW, LOVE ME TONIGHT, THE BIG POND, THE LOVE PARADE, INNOCENTS OF PARIS, GONZAGUE and TROP CREDULES.

FRED ASTAIRE was born in 1899 and he died in 1987. He was a multi-talented actor. He was a famous dancer. He acted and sang. He also was a choreographer. Fred Astaire began acting in the 1930s. He was an excellent dresser and he wore a top hat. Astaire entered show biz as a dancer when he was a boy. Astaire went to Hollywood and signed up with RKO Pictures. The next year he went to MGM for DANCING LADY. He returned to RKO for FLYING DOWN TO RIO, his first movie with Ginger Rogers. FRED ASTAIRE'S career went into high gear in the mid-1930s with TOP HAT and SHALL WE DANCE. He starred in GHOST STORY, THE TOWERING INFERNO, SILK STOCKINGS, FUNNY FACE, BAND WAGON, THE BELLE OF NEW YORK, LET'S DANCE, THREE LITTLE WORDS, THE BARKLEY'S OF BROADWAY, EASTER PARADE, BLUE SKIES, YOLANDA AND THE THIEF, HOLIDAY INN, YOU'LL NEVER GET RICH, THE STORY OF VERNON AND IRENE CASTLE, CAREFREE, A DAMSEL IN DISTRESS, SHALL WE DANCE?, SWING TIME, FOLLOW THE FLEET, TOP HAT, ROBERTA, THE GAY DIVORCEE and FLYING DOWN TO RIO.

Fred Astaire retired in the 1960s. He made rare TV appearances such as DR. KILDARE, etc. Astaire appeared as Chameleon on the science fiction series BATTLESTAR GALACTICA in 1979.

CHARLES LAUGHTON was born in 1898 and he died in 1962. His star qualities were as follows. He was a director, producer, teacher, writer and innovator. He played a variety of characters such as offbeat, literary and historical characters. Charles Laughton had a British education as well as officer training at the Jesuit School Stonyhurst College before serving in World War I. After the war he trained as an actor at London's Royal Academy of Dramatic Arts.

Laughton is well known for his role as Nero in THE SIGN OF THE CROSS and the title character in THE PRIVATE LIFE OF HENRY VIII which won him an Oscar. Other films Laughton was in are ADVISE AND CONSENT, SPARTACUS, WITNESS FOR THE PROSECUTION, THE STRANGE DOOR, THE SUSPECT, THIS LAND IS MINE, THE HUNCHBACK OF NOTRE DAME, JAMAICA INN, I, CLAUDIUS, REMBRANDT, MUTINY ON THE BOUNTY, RUGGLES OF RED GAB ISLAND OF LOST SOULS and THE OLD DARK HOUSE.

SPENCER TRACY was born in 1900 and he died in 1967. He was a highly versatile and talented actor. He acted in a variety of films with Katherine Hepburn. He was spotted by John Ford, who took him to Hollywood to star in UP THE RIVER in 1930, a comedy. He played some tough guy roles. He appeared in films such as GUESS WHO'S COMING TO DINNER, JUDGMENT AT NUREMBURG, INHERIT THE WIND, THE OLD MAN AND THE SEA, BAD DAY AT BLACK ROCK, FATHER OF THE BRIDE, BOYS TOWN, CAPTAINS COURAGEOUS, SAN FRANCISCO, 20,000 YEARS IN SING SING, QUICK MILLIONS, ADAM'S RIB, STATE OF THE UNION, THE SEA OF GRASS, THE SEVENTH CROSS, WOMAN OF THE YEAR, STANLEY AND LIVINGSTONE, FURY, IT'S A MAD MAD MAD WORLD and EDWARD MY SON.

HELEN HAYES was born in 1900 and she died in 1993. She was known as "The First Lady of the American Theater." She was a child star of the stage and leading lady of drama. She had a long acting career. She also was a writer. To Broadway audiences of the 1920s and 1930s, Helen Hayes was the most important actress in America and throughout the twentieth century. She began acting at the age of five. She continued acting until the age of eighty-five. She received four U.S. entertainment awards, an Oscar, Emmy and

Grammy. She acted in CANDLESHOE, AIRPORT, ONE OF OUR DINOSAURS IS MISSING, HERBIE RIDES AGAIN, VANESSA, HER LOVE STORY, WHAT EVERY WOMAN KNOWS, NIGHT FLIGHT, ANOTHER LANGUAGE, THE WHITE SISTER, THE SON-DAUGHTER, A FAREWELL TO ARMS, ARROWSMITH, THE SIN OF MADELONG CLAUDET, THE DANCING TOWN and THE WEAVERS OF LIFE. Hayes played a grand dame in the 1950s, notably as Ingrid Bergman's grandmother in the DOWAGER EXPRESS, as Maria Feodorouna in ANASTASIA in 1956. She won her second Oscar in Best Supporting Actress for her role as a stowaway in AIRPORT in 1970. She died at age 92.

JEAN ARTHUR was born in 1900 and died in 1991. She was a comedienne, and she played innocent, shy and sophisticated roles as an actress. Jean started as a model. Then she made her film debut in the silent cameo KIRBY in 1923. When talkies arrived Jean played comedy and drama equally well. She had a prominent role opposite Edward G. Robinson in John Ford's gangster comedy THE WHOLE TOWN'S TALKING in 1935. She performed in MR. DEEDS GOES TO TOWN in 1936 and MR. SMITH GOES TO WASHINGTON in 1939. In each scenario she befriended the naïve hero and defends him against the crooks and cynics seeking to destroy him. Director Frank Capra described Jean as "my favorite actress." Jean Arthur acted in SHANE A FOREIGN AFFAIR, THE MORE THE MERRIER, THE TALK OF THE TOWN, THE DEVIL AND MISS JONES, TOO MANY HUSBANDS, ONLY ANGELS HAVE WINGS, YOU CAN'T TAKE IT WITH YOU, EASY LIVING, HISTORY IS MADE AT NIGHT, MORE THAN A SECRETARY and THE PLAINSMAN. She had a TV series, THE JEAN ARTHUR SHOW in 1966. It ran for only 11 weeks. She then retired from the screen world and turned her talents to teaching at Vassar College and North Carolina School of the Arts.

CLARK CABLE was born in 1901 and he died in 1960. He had charisma and a powerful voice. He was handsome, charming and known to be a lady's man. Clark Gable was nicknamed "The King of Hollywood" in the 1930s he reigned as the epitome of on-screen masculinity. He wooed women. He played a lead role in GONE WITH THE WIND in 1939. He acted in RED DUST, wooing Jean Harlow and Mary Astor. Then he worked for MGM and worked with

Joan Crawford in DANCING LADY and HOLD YOUR MAN. He costarred with Claudette Colbert in IT HAPPENED ONE NIGHT. Other films Clark Gable acted in are THE MISFITS, RUN SILENT RUN DEEP, THE TALL MEN, LONE STAR, COMMAND DECISION, SAN FRANCISCO, MUTINY ON THE BOUNTY, THE CALL OF THE WILD, MANHATTAN MELODRAMA, NO MAN OF HER OWN, THE SECRET SIX and THE FINGER POINTS.

There are other prominent stars who have made a name in the film industry. These stars are Robert Taylor, Elizabeth Taylor, Gabby Hayes, Walter Brennan, Alan Ladd, Kathryn Hepburn, Montgomery Clift, Greer Garson, Jeanette McDonald, Shelley Winters, Olivia De Haveland, Judy Garland, Cary Grant, Gregory Peck, Gary Cooper, Van Johnson, Esther Williams, Dick Powell, Eleanor Powell, Jane Wyman, Howard Keel, Kathryn Grayson, Marilyn Monroe, Fred McMurray, Claudette Colbern, Gene Kelly, Robert Redford, Barbara Streisand, Gene Kelly and more. Movies are still being produced around the world.

Orlando Bloom, Sean Penn, Drew Barrymore, Mel Gibson, the two leading stars of the blockbuster movie TITANIC (Leonardo DiCaprio and Kate Winslet), Brad Pitt (SEVEN YEARS IN TIBET), and Cameron Diaz are contemporary actresses and actors.

SIXTY-ONE

ART LINKLETTER, BROADCASTER, AUTHOR AND ENTREPRENEUR

Art Linkletter was a broadcaster, author and entrepreneur. He hosted the Art Linkletter Show on television in 1952 to 1970. Another name for the television show was House Party. Art Linkletter asked children unusual and interesting questions.

Art Linkletter wrote a book entitled "KIDS SAY THE DARNEDEST THINGS" which became a very popular book. He also wrote several sequels. "The idea to showcase children's, unrehearsed comments came to him during a conversation with his oldest child, Jack after the boy's first day in kindergarten," Art Linkletter stated.

Informed by Art's son, Jack that he would never go back to school, his father asked why. Jack responded, "Because I can't read, I can't write and they won't let me talk." Art Linkletter decided to interview different children so that they could speak candidly. House Party debuted on CBS radio first before a TV program was established for more than 25 years. The Canadian-born Art Linkletter hosted, "People Are Funny" and the Emmy award winning "House Party" on radio and television for more than 25 years. Art Linkletter last regularly appeared on TV as a contributor on "Kids Say The Darndest Things", a half hour show that Bill Cosby hosted.

Art Linkletter, who as National Easter Seals Chairman, posed with Easter Seals twins, Patricia and Paula Webber and President Kennedy in 1961. Art Linkletter is a prolific author who has written six books featuring cute quotes from kids. He has also tackled drug abuse, salesmanship and public speaking. His 1960 autobiography was called "CONFESSIONS OF A HAPPY MAN."

After co-writing the anti-aging book "HOW TO MAKE THE REST OF YOUR LIFE THE BEST OF YOUR LIFE", in 2006, Art Linkletter signed 400 copies in one book signing during a book tour in 2008. He lectured more than 60 times a year and he continued to run Linkletter Enterprises.

Art Linkletter was abandoned as an infant. He was adopted by an elderly, itinerant evangelist and cobbler, John Linkletter and his wife, Mary Linkletter. They moved to California, when he was a young child. After graduating from high school at 16, Art Linkletter did odd jobs around the United States. He worked as a busboy in Chicago, a stevedore in New Orleans, a meat packer in Minneapolis, a coupon clerk on Wall Street during the 1929 crash and a shipboard laborer between New York and Buenos Aires.

Art Linkletter enrolled at San Diego State College. In his Junior year, Linkletter was hired as an announcer at San Diego Radio Station KGB. After graduating with his B.A. degree in English and Psychology in 1934, he turned down a teaching job to stick with announcing because it paid more.

Art Linkletter was successful as a radio announcer. He was named program director of the California International Exposition in San Diego in 1935 and radio director of the Texas Centennial Exposition in 1936. He took the same job a year later at the San Francisco World Fair. In 1942, Linkletter moved to Hollywood where he excelled in creating and starring in audience-participation shows. He worked with John Guedel, who had created "People Are Funny." Linkletter pioneered zany stunts and interviews that became the prototype for radio and television's now familiar game shows and reality.

In 1955, Linkletter served as the primary host of Disneyland's opening day ceremonies. Walt Disney said he could pay Art Linkletter only by the union scale. Linkletter asked for and received exclusive rights to the camera and film concession at Disneyland for a decade.

"I always wanted to be a star." Art Linkletter once said as he assessed his strengths. He said, "I had no talent. But the most important talent you can have in television is to be liked. People liked me. Secondly, I sincerely and truly liked people and I was curious about their answers. Even the jerks—I wanted to know what made them such jerks."

Art Linkletter became a wealthy businessman. He invented hula hoops, delved into oil wells, invested in lead mines, manufacturing plants, restaurants, television productions, real estate, Australian sheep and cattle stations, construction, mobile storage units and even a bowling alley, a skiing rink and a charm school.

Linkletter became a philanthropist. As he became older, Linkletter worked to serve the seniors as president of the UCLA Center on Aging, national spokesman for the senior lobbying group now known as USA Next and board chairman of the John Douglas French Alzheimer's Foundation.

Art Linkletter lost two of his five children because of early deaths. He became a national spokesman on drug abuse after his youngest child, Diane jumped to her death from her Hollywood apartment in 1969 at the age of twenty, because she was on LSD. He and his daughters had won a Grammy for their spoken word recording "We Love You. Call Collect." An emotional father-daughter conversation recorded not long before her death.

In 1980, Linkletter's second son, Robert was killed at 35 in a car crash. His eldest son, Jack, who followed his father into broadcasting and worked in the family business empire, died at 70 of lymphoma in 2007.

Linkletter served on the President's National Advisory Council for Drug Abuse Prevention, and was president of the National Coordinating Council on Drug Abuse Education and Information.

Linkletter skied until he was 92. He was vigorous and experienced longevity. He was so optimistic about his own future that he signed a contract to lecture in Washington D.C. on his 100th birthday, July 12th, 2012. In addition to his wife of 75 years, Linkletter is survived by daughters Dawn Griffin and Sharon Linkletter, seven grandchildren and 15 great grandchildren.

SIXTY-TWO
SEDONA, A SPIRITUAL PLACE

Sedona, Arizona is a place of awesome beauty and an extraordinary energy is felt by every person wandering through its red-rock canyons. Dick Sutphen went to Sedona in 1969. He said, "I instantly knew this was a special place, not only because of its special place, not only because of its magnificent beauty, but because of an undeniable, spiritual vibration emanating throughout the area. Over the years, I've become convinced, through my own experiences and the experiences of others and through extensive research and investigation, that the psychic energy here is greater than anywhere else in the country."

In RELIGION OF THE RED MOUNTAIN by Heather Hughes, she said "Indian legend tells us that there are four places in the world designated as "power spots" and that these four are broken into two plus two—two positive and two negative or two "light" and two "dark". It is believed that the two "positive" places in the world are Kauai, an island in Hawaii and Sedona, both red-rock country. Sedona and Kauai, the Indians say, are vortexes of energy in which the Great Spirit gives birth to rainbows.

"Indians tell us that the towering crimson peaks stimulate sensitivity and that here a man realizes his true dreams and ambitions. They also say that the mountains are like a great magnet and that people are drawn to them because it is the home of the Great Spirit. Amid red-rock country, it is said that man comes face to face with himself and

the potentials of his nature," according to Dick Sutphen who wrote
SEDONA: PSYCHIC ENERGY VORTEXES.

Dick Sutphen conducted a Psychic Seminar in Sedona. The results
were incredible. Seminars are conducted once or twice yearly ever
since. Seminar participants have reported phenomenal experiences
while meditating or using self hypnosis in these environments. The
experiences range from intense spiritual visions to impressions of what
took place in these canyons long ago. Many of the participants have
reported physical healings. For most newcomers generate a physical
change that naturally eliminates the need for sleep. Some vortex
experiences are transforming, spiritual and totally renewing.

An ancient city existed in the area that is now Sedona. Many people
have related visions of energy fields generated by crystals, advanced
civilizations or extraterrestrial beings who escaped destruction. There
was an ancient Lemurian city buried beneath the great, red-rock
formations and canyons that now comprise the terrain.

According to Churchward, Lemuria was a huge Pacific continent
unconnected to what is now the North American continent. Lemurians
were a spiritual, peaceful people. They developed a very just and fair
governmental system.

Great cataclysms took place approximately 80,000 years ago the
final cataclysms took place 12,000 years ago and sent Mu and millions
of the inhabitants to the depths of the sea in a "vortex of fire and water."
The Lemurians were warned, so they established colonies in areas such
as Egypt, Peru, Central America and Mexico.

The Lemurians had some great rulers. One was a woman. This
civilization consisted of highly skilled artisans and craftsmen. They
enjoyed a very advanced form of civilization with great cities and
impressive temples. Many Lemurians attained a Universal perspective.
There is little scientific argument that a great land mass once existed
above the water in the Pacific, where only Lemurian mountaintops
remain today as islands. In the Mexican temple of Uxmal, an inscription
declares that the temple was dedicated to the memory of Mu, "the lands
in the west, that land of Kui, the birthplace of our sacred mysteries.
The temple faces west, the direction of the lost continent," stated Dick
Sutphen.

Ruth Montgomery, who wrote THE WORLD BEFORE, used
automatic writing to receive messages from her guides. She stated

that Easter Island in the Pacific marks the site of a great, Lemurian, ceremonial center. In Edgar Cayce's reading #812-1, the "sleeping prophet" talked about a woman named Amelia, a priestess in the temple of Light, who was an overseer of communications between various lands. The reading mentions Mu and a particular portion of Arizona and Nevada that are a portion of the Brotherhood of those people from Mu", stated Dick Sutphen.

According to Churchward, "Lemuria was known as The Land of The Sun" and "Empire of The Sun." Churchward, in his book THE SACRED SYMBOLS OF MU, claims that the cliff-dwelling Indians of Arizona and New Mexico were once residents of Lemuria.

The Hopi Indian reservation and mesas are close to Sedona. Hopi legend claims tribes came to the current area from the West after their world was destroyed. They traveled on bamboo rafts until they came to a wall of steep mountains which they climbed. As they looked back, they could see islands sinking behind them.

Lemuria also existed in California and extended to Arizona. Lemuria was a very large continent which existed a million years ago. At least three- fourths of Lemuria sank into the ocean during earthquakes and volcanic eruptions. There were many temples and advanced civilizations on Lemuria. The creative fire was misused. As a result, most of Lemuria was destroyed and fell into the ocean. Sedona in Arizona, Mount Shasta in California and the Central Coast of California remain where Lemuria existed. The high force field of energy in these locations should be maintained.

SIXTY-THREE
HEALING HERB REMEDIES

Herbal remedies are available to heal different ailments and diseases. THE A To Z GUIDE TO HEALING HERBAL REMEDIES by Jason Elias, M.A. L.Ac and Shelagh Ryan Masline who have written about the natural way to good health in a valuable book.

Eyebright is used to treat eye ailments and for people with chronic allergies or sinus infections.

Fo-Ti is a Chinese longevity tonic, which gives energy and strength. It is rejuvenating for the elderly. It is an aphrodisiac and it keeps hair from turning grey.

Paul D'Arco is native to Brazil. This is one of nature's best fungus fighters. It makes a fabulous, natural alternative for treating athlete's foot and vaginal yeast infections. It also shows it may have anti-cancer potential.

Red Clover has anti-tumor properties. It has long had a reputation as an immune-enhancer and for being a wonderful remedy for skin problems such as eczema, especially in children.

Slippery Elm is soothing for sore throats. The mucilage in this popular herb helps to ease digestive problems such as duodenal ulcers, enteritis, gastritis and diarrhea

Other herbs which cure diseases and ailments are agnus-castus which alleviates many menstrual problems including PMS. It counters many of the unpleasant symptoms of menopause, including hot flashes, night sweats and anxiety. Agnuscastus naturally stimulates progesterome. Agnus-castus may be effective in reducing fibroid tumors. Agnus-castus may increase milk production in nursing mothers.

Agrimony is an astringent herb that has binding qualities that can stop bleeding. Agrimony is used to treat urinary infections and infections of the intestinal tract. It is a restorative tonic to the stomach. Ointments made from agrimony may shrink your hemorrhoids and soothe sores and insect bites.

Alfalfa is a nutritious and restorative tonic. Alfalfa is rich in beta-caratene, vitamins C, D. E and K and minerals such as calcium, potassium and bron. The Arabs who discovered alfalfa named it "the father of all foods" Alfalfa is an excellent, overall tonic. It boosts your normal vitality and strength. It is helpful during convalescence or anemia. New research suggests that alfalfa may reduce blood cholesterol levels and plaque deposits which precede heart disease and strokes. Alfalfa may neutralize carcinogens in the colon. Alfalfa may be used to treat acute or chronic cystitus. Alfalfa can relieve inflammation of the prostrate. Alfalfa may relieve lower back pain and reduce bloating or water retention and relieve constipation. Alfalfa leaves are more significant than sprouts in herbal healing. Alfalfa sprouts are delicious in salads.

Almond plants provide us with a safe and natural alternative to dry, commercial soaps and shampoos. Oil made from almonds has natural skin, nourishing qualities. Research indicates that almond oil helps to lower your total cholesterol level. Almond soaps can clean your skin without making it dry. Almond oils and lotions will soften and moisturize your skin. Cooking with almond oil may reduce your cholesterol level. Almond products are commonly available in commercial form as nut kernels, oils, lotions and butters.

Aloe Vera is a versatile herb. It has been used for more than 3,500 years. Aloe Vera taken internally relieves constipation and benefits the liver. The gel taken from this leaf of the aloe plant is one of nature's greatest moisturizers. In Ayurvedic medicines aloe vera gel is known as estrogenic, or having significant tonic and restorative qualities for women. In Sanskrit the gel is called kumari. The translation is "goddess" which refers to its tonic, anti-aging value for women. Aloe can relieve sunburn and promote the healing of other kinds of minor burns and skin irritations. Aloe vera can relieve radiation burns suffered by patients undergoing chemotherapy. Aloe vera is a laxative and a restorative to the liver. Aloe vera helps to slow the development of wrinkles.

Artichokes can be eaten freshly steamed. Artichokes stimulate the flow of bile from the liver and are used in the treatment of liver disease. They have also been utilized in some forms of kidney diseases, diabetes mellitus and atherosclerosis. Artichokes can reduce your cholesterol level. The artichoke is a natural diuretic, which means that eating artichokes can help you to reduce excess water weight. Use the stems, leaves and roots of the artichokes.

Asparagus root is used for its diuretic qualities. It increases the flow of urine. It is a urinary tract soother and tonic. Asparagus root is a nutritive tonic that relieves some of the symptoms of chronic fatigue syndrome, tuberculosis and even AIDS. Asparagus root is a restorative tonic for the female reproductive system. Asparagus root may enhance fertility, relieve menstrual cramps and increase the flow of breast milk in nursing women. Asparagus root is an effective treatment for urinary tract infections and kidney stones. Asparagus root may relieve painful swelling associated with rheumatism. Asparagus root is a nutritive tonic for the lungs, making this herb useful in alleviating some of the wasting system of tuberculosis and AIDS.

Balm of Gilead is an herb taken from tall poplar trees and used in the treatment of coughs and upper respiratory infections. This herb helps to clear mucous membranes. Balm of Gilead can relieve laryngitis coughs and sore throats Balm of Gilead is a soothing and disinfecting expectorant. Balm of Gilead is used in the treatment of bronchial and upper respiratory infections. Balm of Gilead is most commonly available in commercial form as a syrup or tincture.

Barberry, known as jaundice berry, contains the infection fighting constituent berberine. Its antibiotic qualities make barberry valuable in the treatment of ailments such as sore throat, diarrhea and urinary-tract treatments. Barberry is good for gall bladder infections and liver problems. Barberry is a good tonic for digestion. Barberry stimulates the immune system. Barberry may be helpful in relieving the symptoms of liver diseases such as hepatitis, jaundice and chronic liver disease. Barberry may help to detoxify the liver as in the cases of alcoholism, poor diet or drug abuse. Barberry may relieve spleen enlargement and some chronic stomach problems.

Blessed Thistle is a traditional, folk remedy, used in the treatment of stomach, liver, lung and kidney problems. Blessed Thistle is used by women to correct the hormonal imbalances that cause irregular menstrual disorders and cycles. Blessed Thistle can improve your appetite, stimulate your memory and act as a tonic for your circulation and digestion. Blessed thistle can improve your digestion and relieve stomach cramps, indigestion and gas. Blessed thistle can stimulate your appetite. Blessed thistle helps to lower fevers and stops bleeding and resolves blood clots.

Catnip is effective in the treatment of colds and fevers. Europeans have used this herb for diarrhea and bronchitis. Catnip is recommended for hyperactive children. The flowers and leaves are used. Catnip has a calming, soothing influence on the nervous system. Use it to relieve stress and nervous tension. Catnip helps to cure insomnia. Catnip products are most commonly available in commercial form as capsules, tinctures and teas.

Chamomile is one of the most popular herbs used in the United States today. Europeans have used chamomile as a natural herbal remedy for stress and insomnia. It is used to relieve painful menstrual cramps, indigestion and back pain. Chamomile poultice can ease the discomfort of cramps and sore muscles. Chamomile extract is used to treat skin irritations. Chamomile is a safe and helpful way to relieve every day tension and stress. Chamomile is used to treat many conditions caused by stress such as indigestion, a nervous stomach and diarrhea. A weak preparation of chamomile tea is generally a safe remedy for calming irritable children and it is used to treat kidney and bladder problems.

Chaparral is a powerful antibiotic. Chaparral helps to prevent the cell damage and abnormalities that many experts believe eventually cause cancer. Chaparral should be used with caution and only under professional supervision. Chaparral is a powerful, natural antibiotic, making it an effective treatment for infections caused by bacteria, viruses and parasites.

Cloves have been used by the Chinese for over two thousand years. Cloves are a remedy of Ayurvedic healers in India for the treatment of respiratory and digestive disorders. Scientists have discovered that cloves are rich in chemical eugenal which is the source of its anesthetic and antiseptic qualities. Clove oil is used as a Lavaris mouthwash. Cloves have a warming and stimulating effect on your body. Clove oil is commonly used externally to relieve painful toothaches. A few drops of clove oil in warm water can relieve nausea and vomiting. Cloves are used to treat digestive disorders. Cloves are a restorative tonic to your digestion and circulation. Cloves are often added to bitter herb remedies to make them taste better. Clove products are most commonly available in commercial form as oils, infusions, extracts and capsules.

Cranberry is used by women as a natural way to prevent urinary tract infections. Cranberry products are most commonly available in commercial form as juices, extracts and capsules. Avoid sugar-laden, commercial brands of cranberry juice. Buy bottles of pure cranberry juice at health food stores and dilute with water.

Dandelion is a valuable and nutritious herb widely used in Europe today and has been popular in ancient cultures dating back to the ancient Chinese and Ayurvedic healers. Dandelion leaves are a natural diuretic, which helps to increase the flow of urine. The dandelion root is a helpful liver tonic. Dandelions are packed with valuable antioxidants such as vitamins A and C. Scientists believe that antioxidants can prevent abnormal cell activity that often precedes cancer. Dandelion is a digestive aid and may reduce the level of sugar in your blood. Try taking a little dandelion before your period. It helps to relieve the bloating that often precedes it. Dandelion stimulates the flow of bile. It is a good tonic. Dandelion, used as a diuretic, helps to lower high blood pressure and stop congestive heart failure. It is a good tonic for your liver and gallbladder and an effective treatment for liver disorders such as jaundice.

Echinacea is a traditional, North American remedy with enormous, immune boosting and healing qualities. Echinacea strengthens your body's tissues and protects you from the attack of harmful germs. Take Echinacea at the beginning of each season to ward off infection. Echinacea extract increases production of infection fighting T cells. Echinacea is used to fight off colds, flu, bronchitis, tonsillitis, tuberculosis and meningitis. Echinacia helps to heal wounds and is used to treat cuts, burns, eczema and psoriasis because of its blood-cleaning abilities. When Echinacea is taken with antifungal creams it helps to lessen vaginal yeast infection. Echinacea products are most commonly available in commercial form as capsules, tinctures, decoctions and axtractions. Echinacea is generally a very safe herb. Side effects are rare.

Eucalyptus, is known as Australian gum, blue gum and in gum tree. It is used as a cold and flu remedy. Eucalyptus is an effective treatment for upper-respiratory ailments; notably colds, flu and bronchitis. Eucalyptol is an active ingredient in many products such as Vicks, VapoRub, Dristan decongestant and Sine-Off. Eucalyptus is a good expectorant. Simply inhaling it loosens the phlegm in your chest. Eucalyptus is a powerful, natural antiseptic. It may be useful in treating minor cuts or scrapes. Use eucalyptus ointment to relieve painful arthritis and rheumatism. Eucalyptus products are most commonly available in commercial form as liniments, oils and leaves.

Ginkgo Biloba has a unique ability to inhibit a process called platelet activity factor (PAF). PAF plays a major role in your body's processes; such as blood flow and blood clots. By blocking PAF ginkgo exhibits tremendous healing possibilities. Ginkgo helps to prevent strokes that occur when blood flow to the brain is blocked. Heart attacks may be prevented if ginkgo biloba is taken.

Ginseng is primarily grown in Wisconsin, America. It was traditionally used by Native Americans to treat nausea and vomiting. American ginseng is used around the world. Ginseng helps people to deal with emotional and physical stress. Ginseng can increase your resistance to disease by stimulating your immune system. Ginseng is an excellent, overall tonic for your body. Ginseng counteracts fatigue. Ginseng may improve physical stamina. Ginseng stimulates one's appetite, which can be especially useful for the elderly.

Several studies have indicated that ginseng reduces your total blood cholesterol level. Ginseng has an anti-clotting action that may reduce your risk of heart-attacks. Ginseng may be used by diabetics to reduce their blood sugar level. Be sure to consult a physician before using ginseng in your regular treatment regimen. Ginsing is often recommended by herbalists for the treatment of respiratory problems. Ginseng may enhance liver function. Ginseng can improve your concentration and memory.

There are many more herbs which can improve your health such as Goldenseal, Gotu Kola, Hawthorn, Hops, Horse Chestnut, Juniper, Lady's Mantle, Lemon Balm, Licorice, Lobella, Marigold, Meadowsweet, Milk Thistle, Motherwort, Mullein, Myrrh, Oats, Papaya, Parsley, Peppermint, Plantain, Psyllium, Red Clover, Rosemary, St. John's Wort, Saw Palmetto, Slippery Elm, Thyme, Uva-Ursi,

Valerian, Vervain, White Willow, Wild Cherry Bark, Wild Indigo, Witch Hazel, Wood Betony, Yarrow and Yellow Dock.

Natural herbs are very useful and helpful in aiding people to overcome diseases and ailments. There are no side effects and harmful, man-made substances added to natural herbs.

SIXTY-FOUR

PLANET X FORECAST
AND MORE ABOUT 2012

Zecharia Sitchin, well known author and researcher, wrote about Planet X which he had read about in THE KOLBIN BIBLE, a well documented book of ancient folk law and wisdom texts from around the globe. Egyptians called Planet X the Destroyer as do passages in THE HOLY BIBLE, The Druid ancestors of the Celts called Planet X, the Frightener.

Many Planet X researchers believe that Planet X was unofficially imaged for the first time for the first time in 1983 by NASA's infrared Astronomical Satellite (IRAS). A highly sophisticated infrared observatory, the SPT became operational in early 2007. Year-Month Solar Observatory specialized in the study of planetary threats and space debris and it is located in the North West Cape of Western Australia.

Planet X is most likely a Brown Dwarf in an unstable orbit. It could very well be that Planet X is a brown dwarf that was once in unstable orbit along the ecliptic. Then something caused it to enter into a sharply perpendicular orbit that is now degrading. Earth's orbit is not a perfect circle so it is described as being elliptical (comet-like). At aphelion, it visits a distant region of our solar system where no spacecraft has ever traveled. At perihelion, it passes through the asteroid belt between Mars and Jupiter.

Planet X has an inclined orbit that lies in a plane that is almost perpendicular to the ecliptic. It enters the inner solar systemand it will cross the plane of the ecliptic shortly before it reaches perihelion where its most violent inter actions with the Sun will occur.

After Planet X crosses the ecliptic intense, electrical, interactions with the sun will begin, causing it to become extremely violent. Once Planet X reaches perihelion, the interaction will become even more severe and we will see sprites (cosmic lightning) between the two bodies. As Planet X heads back out to the edge of our system, the Sun will begin to settle down.

Planet X is approaching the inner solar system for a near future fly by. We know this by the way this object is inter acting with familiar objects in our solar system, such as the Sun and planets. Planet X became visible in 2010.

In 2006, a large infrared telescope became operational at the South Pole. In mid 2009, Planet X was clearly visible at night as a bright reddish object to those in the Southern Hemisphere looking through backyard telescopes and high powered binoculars. By continuously observing Planet X for erratic behavior or changes in its orbit, scientists will be better able to determine how it will interact with our sun during the 2012 flyby. It is predicted that Planet X will pass through an ecliptic plane and will trigger strong electrical interaction with the Sun. This object will appear as a second sun. It will be bright red and approximately the size of the moon.

Cataclysm possibilities in 2012 are asteroid impacts with tsunamis. Major earthquakes with tsunamis may occur. Volcanic eruptions may take place on December 21st, 2012. People around the world should prepare for cataclysms super volcanoes, magnitude 9+ earthquakes along major fault lines as well as tsunamis. Global weather patterns will become violent. Part of our atmosphere may become ionized and become poisonous to breathe. Entire regions may become poisonous to all forms of life. Earth's power grids, transportation systems and communications networks will be destroyed.

People should prepare to live underground for a long period of time until the Earth is restored. The atmosphere will need to be purified and life on Earth such as people. Plants and animals and sea life will need to move to survive. Let us hope that Planet X moves far enough away from Earth so that cataclysms do not affect mother Earth and humanity can survive.

Jacco Van Der Worp, MS, Mashall Masters and Janice Manning wrote: Planet X Forecast and 2012 Survival Guide have done extensive research about Planet X and about forecasts about 2012.

SIXTY-FIVE
CHOCOLATE CAN HEAL YOU

Chocolate has healthy benefits including decreased blood pressure, lower cholesterol, reduced risk of heart disease; even effects on moods. Evidence linking consumption of chocolate or cocoa to better health first emerged more than ten years ago from studies of Kuna people, natives of San Blas Islands off the coast of Panama.

Studies of the Kuna were made in the 1990's The Kuna's have found that they had lower blood pressure, better kidney function and lower blood pressure, better kidney function and lower rates of heart disease and cancer compared with other Panamanians

A 1997 study indicated that only 2% of Kuna's living on the San Blas Island had high blood pressure compared with 10% of Kuna Panamanians living in Panama City where the Kuna's had largely abandoned their traditional diet. The Kuna diet included 5 to 7 cups of cocoa-based drinks which were loaded with a flavonoid compound, an antioxidant-a-day of flavonul chocolate. Those who ate the dark chocolate, the diameter of their coronary arteries increased to 2.51 millimeters. Where as in the other group their artery diameter was unchanged at 2.36 mm. Platelets were less likely to stick in the artery walls of those who ate the dark chocolate, the researchers found. This 2007 study was published in the 2007 Journal CIRCULATION.

Julia Zumppano, a clinical dietitian in the department of preventative cardiology, Cleveland Ohio, recommended no more than an ounce of 70% dark chocolate per day and half of that for those losing weight. Dark not milk or white chocolate is dense in flavanoids.

Various studies indicate that a certain amount of dark chocolate without sugar and without milk, is good for you. Dark, unsweetened chocolate helps you to avoid heart trouble and high blood pressure.

SIXTY-SIX

ABOUT JERRY BROWN AS A CALIFORNIA GOVERNOR

Jerry Brown was a governor in California in the 1970s. He is running as a California candidate as governor again. He has a reputation for helping agriculture because he supported the farmers. He also helped to improve the economy in California.

Jerry Brown's father, Pat Brown, was a California governor in the 1960s for 12 years. He was known to be a good governor. He stabilized the economy and he spoke up about major issues. He followed through with his political promises.

Jerry Brown is running for California governor again in 2010. "In his first major appearances since winning the Democratic primary, gubernatorial candidate Jerry Brown spoke to an enthusiastic crowd of teachers preaching the need for frugality and innovation," stated Carla Rivera, a columnist for Los Angeles Times. Brown has cast himself as the candidate with the ability to mobilize a polarized electorate to regain the public's trust.

Jerry Brown called for teacher-initiated reform. He spoke about the federal government's Race to the Top initiative and its emphasis on testing and data collection. Brown spoke of the need to improve teacher training and to fix social and economic barriers that hamper learning. "He's a strong advocate for education and knows what's going on in the classroom and that it's not just about numbers and tests, but teaching the whole child," said Mary Rose Ortega, a third grade teacher at First Street Elementary in Boyle Heights. She said, "He spoke from the heart and understands that improving education is not going to be an easy task."

As an educator I have encouraged my students to think and solve problems. I helped my students to communicate effectively. They worked on individual and group projects which were creative and protective. I taught creative writing, drama, music, art as well as reading, writing and arithmetic. Current events were presented on a daily basis. Committee work was a way to simulate learning skills. Committee members gathered research and developed visual materials to present to the class. I had my students participate in variety shows, skits and original stage plays.

I advocate that teachers use academic skills and integrate classroom curriculum so students can learn as much as possible. If Jerry Brown is elected as a California governor, I hope he will improve the California Budget. Enough money in the California Budget should be allotted for education in California for educational supplies and teacher employment and teacher salaries. It is my opinion that administrators in education are making too much money on an annual basis. This means a lot more money from the California Budget is paid to administrators. Much more money should be reserved to hire teachers and to provide salaries for teachers. Administration salaries should be reduced so more money will be reserved to hire more teachers. I hope Jerry Brown will make these changes in the California Budget so that enough teachers can be employed to serve California students if he is elected as our next California governor.

SIXTY-SEVEN

A BETTER WAY OF LIVING

We can cultivate a better way of living by changing our style of life. How you decorate your home affects how you feel about your daily environment. Surround the interior of your home with colorful, creative and artistic paintings, knickknacks, displays, furniture and plants. Keep your home uncluttered and clean. You will feel much better when you enjoy your home environment.

You will feel better if your home is surrounded with a beautiful garden. Fragrant, colorful flowers add to your outdoor environment. Place patio tables and comfortable chairs near your fragrant garden. You can relax in the privacy of your garden in your outdoor patio.

Soft, relaxing background music can help you relax. Listen to birds chirping outdoors. Select quality TV programs and videos to enjoy while you are at home. Select a variety of stimulating and worthwhile books to read on a regular basis.

Developing interesting hobbies adds to a better way of life. You can play miniature golf in your backyard. Volleyball and Badminton are other outdoor activities to participate in. You can sit at a patio table to play cards, scrabble, checkers and chess.

Set up an easel in your patio so you can paint. You can paint your garden and background scenery. Still life bowls of fruit and flowers can also be painted.

A pond adds an interesting centerpiece to your garden. Lilies can grow in your pond. Be sure to put goldfish and carp in your pond. Frogs may come into your pond as well. You will be able to observe your goldfish, carp and frogs in your pond. More birds will come into your garden if it is fragrant and beautiful. They chirp as well as look beautiful.

You can experience a better way of living by surrounding yourself with a relaxing, beautiful environment.

SIXTY-EIGHT

HOW RELIGION AFFECTS PEOPLE

There are many world religions. People in each culture believe in certain doctrines, creeds and principles about specific religious philosophies. Each religion affects how people behave. Certain religious beliefs cause believers to react about world problems, issues and personal concerns.

For instance, fundamental Christians believe we have one life. If we sin we must repent or we will go to hell after we pass away. Orthodox Christians believe they must be saved by Jesus Christ. If they are not saved by Jesus Christ they believe they will go to hell. They do not believe in reincarnation and karma. Karma is known as cause and effect. Fundamental Christians do not believe in Metaphysics. They usually refuse to listen to anyone who talks about New Age awareness. Christians tend to be closed minded and afraid to expand their spiritual awareness.

Moslems have strict expectations and Moslem women, as a rule, dress in long gowns with cloth capes which cover their bodies and faces. They generally are escorted by their fathers, brothers and husbands when they are in public. Moslems pray and worship five times a day to Allah. They are strict about what they eat especially during lent or Ramadan. Moslems heckle in the streets by making shaking sounds to alert everyone when they are concerned about important issues. They believe Mohammed was the next prophet after Jesus Christ.

Jews believe in the Islamic faith. They have moved around the Middle East to Europe and America. Jews were in search of the promised land in earlier times. Some have taken over land in earlier times. They believe in Jehovah God their supreme ruler. Jews tend to band together. Some have taken over land wherever they formed settlements. Jews generally seek knowledge and truth. They do not belong to other religious groups. They have their own customs and beliefs. They light candles and have a religious ceremony in their homes on Sabbath which is on Saturday night. They believe they are the chosen people on Earth which makes them superior to others in their minds. However, Jews were persecuted at different times in history. Yet, Jews continue to survive and to multiply and thrive.

Hindus chant, burn candles and give flowers and fruit to the Hindu gods. They tend to be vegetarians. They eat fruit, vegetables and grains. Hindus sing Hindu songs and dance religious movements in a unique manner. Hindus pray regularly first thing in the morning and at different times during the day and in the evenings.

Religions affect how people behave, respond and live. Customs and beliefs affect their attitudes and feelings about life. Religion is an important part of their lives. They make major decisions based on their religious values.

SIXTY-NINE

EVOLUTION OF THE EARTH

Planet Earth is approximately five billion years old. Many scientists believe the Earth was formed after the Big Bang. Different planets come from our Sun and orbit around the Sun. Planet Earth is the third planet from the Sun. The Earth is 93 million miles from the Sun.

The Earth began as a fireball. It took at least a million or more years to cool off on the surface. Volcanic eruptions have occurred because the Earth is still very hot inside. Lava spurts out of volcanoes. Hot lava bubbles around inside the Earth. When lava builds up into pressure points it may eventually spurt out of volcanic openings to flow across landscapes and into the oceans.

Lava has cooled off to form new landscapes on the Earth. New lands can develop into new landscapes. The Earth continues to change and develop so that seven major continents have formed on Earth. There are also many islands which exist on Earth which have risen up from the ocean because of lava erupting to the surface of the Earth above the ocean high enough to form islands.

Some islands exist after major continents fell into the sea. Some islands are much older than other islands. Ancient civilizations have lived on the oldest islands in the world. Anthropologists have made studies of ancient civilizations. Scientists have calculated how Earth has formed.

Each stage of the Earth has been carefully studied. The Earth began as a fireball. Then oceans appeared around the whole Earth. Gradually, one continent appeared at a time until there were seven continents. Ocean life developed first. Sea plants grew in the ocean. Finally, animals existed on the land. Humanity existed on different continents.

Life on Earth continued to evolve. The Earth has continued to evolve step by step over 5 million years. Lemuria was the first continent to fall. Atlantis was the second continent to fall .Other continents may fall because of volcanic eruptions and other cataclysms.

The Earth needs protection from asteroids and Planet X. Planet X is moving closer to the Earth. It may be too close to the Earth by December 21, 2012. Cataclysms may occur such as severe earthquakes and ionization of our atmosphere. Electricity may no longer be in use. Many people may die because of lack of enough water and food. Life on Earth may die out and experience severe changes.

Evolution on Earth may be severely affected by climate changes, severe heat waves and depletion of crops and the death of many animals. The Earth may have to be restored gradually once Planet X moves far enough away from the Earth.

SEVENTY

RAMBLING ON

Sheldon Henderson tended to be a wanderer. He rambled on from one place to another. He was restless and felt the need to seek adventure wherever he could experience it. He was originally from a large ranch in Texas. He was a drifter because he was curious what it was like to live in new places.

Sheldon traveled to a sleepy town in Texas where he observed tumbling weeds. Few people walked down the street. The town of Alvarado was very quiet. Sheldon walked into the only café in town. Only two people were in the café beside the waitress and cook. They were sitting at a corner table drinking coffee. Sheldon sat down at a booth near a window.

Music was playing from a juke box. Sheldon waited for the waitress to come to his table. She came to his table with a menu. She brought a glass of cold water with lemon slices. Sheldon glanced at the menu. He decided to order a cheeseburger with lettuce, tomatoes, pickles, catsup, mustard and onion rings.

While Sheldon waited for his cheeseburger and onion rings he drank some coffee. He looked around the café. The music background was the only thing happening. Finally, the cheeseburger and onion rings were brought to Sheldon's table. He began eating them. He thought about moving into a place where there was some action.

Sheldon browsed around Alvarado for several hours after he left the café. He looked into a few stores. He went to the only theater in town. He watched a movie entitled THE SOUND OF MUSIC. He enjoyed this movie. After seeing this film Sheldon felt better. He walked out of the theater and decided to stay overnight in this town.

Sheldon went to the only hotel in downtown Alvarado. He checked into a hotel room. It was approximately 10:30 p.m. He decided to lay down in the hotel bed to rest. It was quiet outside during the night. Sheldon slept well that night. The next morning he woke up, took a shower and dressed in clean clothes. He walked down the street to the only café to eat breakfast. He ordered scrambled eggs, bacon, hash browns and biscuits with butter and jelly. Sheldon sipped hot coffee.

After breakfast, Sheldon left the café and got into his car. He drove out of Alvarado and headed West. He wanted to view more scenery and drove for one hundred miles through tumbleweed and dry countryside. They drove out of Texas into the state of Arizona. He witnessed rich red soil with many pine trees. This countryside was much more interesting.

Once Sheldon got to Flagstaff, Arizona, he stopped his car to rest and fill his car up with gasoline. He noticed that Flagstaff was a bustling city. There were a variety of restaurants, shops and entertainment opportunities. Sheldon decided to stay overnight in Flagstaff. He located a motel and signed in. He went to his motel room and unpacked his traveling bags.

Sheldon walked downtown from his motel to enjoy Flagstaff. He browsed into a large arcade room where there were a variety of arcades. He decided to play at an arcade machine. The games in the machine were fascinating. Sheldon earned points in order to win games. He finally won with a lot of points. He spent $3.00 to play the game by inserting in $3.00 worth of quarters. Then Sheldon played another game. He enjoyed playing baseball on the arcade machines.

When Sheldon was done playing at the arcades he walked outside and continued browsing. He came to an antique shop and looked around in this antique store. He noticed old furniture, lamps, some paintings, old tables, carpets and miscellaneous items. Sheldon noticed the prices were reasonable. He wanted to buy some of the antiques. However, he had no place to keep them in his small car.

Finally, Sheldon left the antique store and continued wandering down the main street. He came to an attractive restaurant. He decided to go in to eat breakfast. He sat at a comfortable table near the main window so he could look outside at what was happening in the street. He ordered a veggie omelet, country potatoes, whole wheat toast and orange juice. He decided not to order coffee.

Sheldon noticed more and more people who came into the restaurant. The restaurant was called the Squeaky Door. A couple sat down near Sheldon approximately fifteen minutes after he arrived. At first, he kept to himself. The couple finally looked over at Sheldon.

The man finally said, "Hello. Have you eaten here before?" Sheldon replied, "No. I am from out of town. I'm traveling around." The man and woman appeared interested in what Sheldon said. The woman spoke. "Where are you traveling to next?" Sheldon replied, "I may be heading out to California. I want to go to San Diego, Los Angeles, Santa Barbara and to San Francisco."

The couple continued to be interested. The man said, "My name is Michael. This is my wife, Michelle." Sheldon responded, "My name is Sheldon. I like to travel around to experience new adventures." Michael remarked, "Good idea. We live in Flagstaff. We plan to take a three weeks vacation every year. We plan to go to the Delaware Valley and the Great Lakes this year. We have been back east to New York and we like to go mountain climbing as well as swimming and boating in different lakes".

Sheldon's breakfast was served by a young, attractive waitress. He began eating his veggie omelet and country potatoes. He sipped his orange juice. He continued to listen to the comments of the couple. Sheldon then replied, "I'm glad you have experienced different adventures. Life is much more interesting when we can experience adventures. I'm planning to head out West to San Diego next. I want to look around Flagstaff first."

After Sheldon finished his breakfast he received his bill. He got up from his table and said goodbye to Michael and Michelle. He said, "It was nice meeting you. Enjoy your trip to the Great Lakes. Goodbye." Michael and Michelle said goodbye. Sheldon paid his bill. He left the restaurant. He continued browsing around Flagstaff.

Sheldon went back to his motel and packed his belongings. He packed his car. Sheldon drove out of Flagstaff and headed West towards San Diego, California. He continued his adventures out West. He planned to travel as long as he could because he was a wanderer who rambled on and on.